Letters to Liesl

ARETÉ

PUBLISHING
USA

Letters to Liesl

by

Charmian Carr
and
Jean Strauss

ARETÉ

PUBLISHING
USA

an Amber/Rose Imprint

Arete Publishing Company of America
an Amber/Rose imprint

P.O. Box 127, Claremont, California 91711 U.S.A.

www.arete-usa.com
www.CharmianCarr.com

LIBRARY OF CONGRESS CATALOGING IN PUBLICATION DATE

Letters to Liesl/ Charmian Carr and Jean Strauss.

1. Carr, Charmian. date. 2. Sound of Music (Motion Picture).
I. Strauss, Jean A. S. II. Title.

ISBN: 0-9627982-1-5

Printed in the United States of America

Cover by Cinnamon Design.
Claremont, California

Dedicated to

Jennifer, Erik, and Emma
and
Emily and Grant

and to Rachel
a drop of golden sun

Contents

When I met Charmian Carr at an event at the Hollywood Bowl in 1998, I asked her endless questions about The Sound of Music. Somehow, she made me feel as if no one had ever asked her what Julie Andrews was like before, or what she enjoyed most about Salzburg, or what were her favorite scenes and songs. Yet, I detected relief in Charmy's eyes when the conductor finally walked on stage, giving her a reprieve from my interrogation, at least until intermission.

I'll never forget what happened next. The orchestra began to play "The Star Spangled Banner", and although I usually sing the anthem with slightly-off-key gusto, I stood silently beside Charmy, listening to her very familiar voice singing those "land of the free" high notes with ease, and it was like stepping into the movie. Her beautiful voice was unchanged despite the passage of thirty-five years, and I couldn't help thinking, "Wow. It's Liesl."

Later that night, as we were saying goodbye, and I was asking just one more question, I grinned and said, "You know, you should write a book about The Sound of Music, and then you wouldn't have to answer all these questions from people like me."

She smiled. "You're the writer. Why don't you write one."

And so I did.

During the months we spent working on Forever Liesl, I would arrive at her house at ten o'clock in the morning and she would make me strong coffee with thick cream (her American version of Austrian café mitschlag) and let me sneak some of her dark chocolate with nuts while I asked her questions and poked through her boxes of memorabilia. She introduced me to her 'film siblings' and to Dan Truhitte (Rolf), to director Bob Wise and screenwriter Ernie Lehman, and arranged a wickedly funny interview with Christopher Plummer.

I found myself wishing, more than once, that I could have met Saul Chaplin. I had never heard of him before I began working on Liesl, but I quickly learned that he was one of those unsung heroes who quietly made magic happen behind the scenes. Saul loved Charmy and was her champion, and as I began to know her, it made me even more fond of him.

Then came the day in the New York hotel when Charmy met the von Trapp "children" for the first time. I knew I was witnessing history. Astoundingly, there was no media involved, just a handful of people who were fortunate to be on hand.

When Charmy introduced me to Maria von Trapp (the second daughter of Georg and his first wife Agathe), I told her the story of my aunt who had seen the Trapp Family Singers perform in Dayton, Ohio in 1940, and how profoundly the audience had been affected when the family ended the performance with "Silent Night" in German. "She told me that it was the most beautiful thing she'd ever heard, and that one-by-one, people in the audience stood up and sang along with you. Many were crying. She said it was a mystical moment, as if you'd touched them with a healing hand. When the song ended, no one clapped. The entire audience stood there, quietly crying, until your family bowed deeply and walked from the stage. My aunt told me she never saw anything more moving in her life."

Maria nodded. "My family hears stories like this all the time, all around the world, and it touches us deeply."

She did not tell me what she and her brothers and sisters were going to do that evening at the ceremony where the Austrian government was honoring both Trapps and the actors who had portrayed them on screen. I sat in the audience unaware that the Trapp Family Singers were going to perform together for the first time in decades and that the first song they were going to sing was "Silent Night" in German.

As they began, Maria glanced over at me in the front row and smiled, and I couldn't hold back my tears. She knew, watching me, that she was giving me a gift of music and memories and cherished people. I shouldn't have been surprised. She is, after all, one of the people who inspired the story of The Sound of Music.

Later, I included my aunt's story in <u>Forever Liesl</u> *when Charmy and I were advised that the twenty-four fan letters from 1965 we intended to place between chapters were unusable without the permission of the letter writers. Finding people via thirty-five year-old addresses posed a daunting task, and Charmy and I were concerned whether we'd succeed.*

And then it happened. Suddenly, every person we spoke with had a "Sound of Music" story, and new letters from fans arrived in Charmy's mailbox, unbidden. Out of thin air, almost overnight, we had twenty-four wonderful stories about people from five to ninety, whose lives were touched and enriched by this one film in ways that I hadn't fathomed possible. The problem was no longer how we would get permission for decades-old letters, but which of the new stories we would use.

Within a week of <u>Forever Liesl</u>'s release, we received a letter asking if Charmy was going to write a sequel. We joked about it at the time, the question striking us as being akin to someone asking a woman who has just given birth when she's going to have another baby. But with the advent of new events in Charmy's life in the new millennium, not to mention in the life of the film itself, it seemed as if another book should be done, not about the making of the movie, but about the unending impact of it.

This book was inspired by thousands of fans who wrote letters and sent stories to Charmy in the wake of her memoir. It is an honor to once again play wordsmith for a film that changed the world and a wonderful woman who will forever be, in the hearts of millions, sixteen-going-on-seventeen.

Jean Strauss

Homeward Bound

Dear Liesl,

When are you and the other 'children' from The Sound of Music *going to do one of those reunion specials? Don't you know how much we all love you?*

Over the years, I've received many letters from fans wanting to see the "von Trapp children" reunited. Now, thirty-six years after we filmed *The Sound of Music*, I sit on a plane bound for Salzburg with Nicholas Hammond (Friedrich), Heather Menzies (Louisa), Duane Chase (Kurt), Angela Cartwright (Brigitta), Debbie Turner (Marta), and Kym Karath (Gretl). En route to doing a British documentary about the making of the film, we have taken over the first two rows of this Austrian Airlines 747, and can't help grinning at each other. We are on a very special adventure, one that we have waited a long time to make, and when Nicky leans over and whispers to me, "This is so cool!", I nod my head in agreement.

Back in 1964, when I sat next to Dan Truhitte (Rolf) during for the long journey across the Atlantic to Austria, my stomach had been filled with butterflies. My whole life had been in front of me back then and I had no idea what the future would bring. I certainly had no inkling that the film we were making would have such an unending and wonderful impact upon all our lives.

Today, much of my life is behind me, and there is much to think about as I look out the window at the ocean below. It has taken the seven of us three-and-a-half decades to return to the city of so many wonderful memories. I'd always believed we'd return to Salzburg one day, but with each passing year, it became clear that orchestrating such a long-distance reunion between seven working adults with families and other obligations, was next to impossible. Life slipped past and it began to appear as if we'd never return. Now here I sit, a grandmother, and we're finally on our way.

In my bag in the overhead bin is a stack of letters, e-mails mostly, sent to me over the past year following the release of my memoir, <u>Forever Liesl</u>. Thousands of people have written to tell me of their love of the film and how it has affected their lives.

I hadn't expected such an outpouring from fans. The film is, after all, decades old. I should have known better. Since *The Sound of Music* first premiered in March of 1965, it has continuously touched people of every generation around the world. We actors get the lion's share of credit, but many talented people were responsible for *The Sound of Music's* success, from composers Rodgers and Hammerstein to director Robert Wise, from associate producer Saul Chaplin and screenwriter Ernest Lehman, to the cinematographers, editors, music directors, set designers, choreographers and puppeteers. Every single person involved in the film contributed to the magic.

Many of them are no longer alive, but six of the people responsible for *The Sound of Music* are seated beside me on this plane, and to me it's nothing short of miraculous that we are able to return to Salzburg after all this time. We have been blessed in our lives in so many ways.

There is something I want to share with these special friends, my second family, something I have learned from these letters. Of course, my six 'film siblings' all receive fan mail. Perhaps my personal epiphany will be nothing new to them. But what I've received has been a revelation to me. At the right moment, I will tell my 'family'.

But for now, it's just wonderful to have some privacy together. So often when we're reunited, we're 'on camera'. When we connected up at Chicago's O'Hare Airport for this flight to Austria, as Heather and Angela and I walked into the lounge where we'd agreed to meet, we were blinded by the klieg lights of a film crew on hand to capture our reunion. It's hard to be natural and spontaneous in such a setting, and it wasn't until we boarded the plane that I felt we were really could be ourselves, laughing and talking non-stop.

Nicky finally leans back in his chair beside me, trying to catch some sleep, exhausted by his long flight from Australia where he now lives, which preceded this flight to Austria. I pull the blanket up around him and lean back in my seat, thinking about this journey.

This is different from any other trip the seven of us have ever made together for one simple reason: we are alone. Back in 1964, Nicky and Heather and Angela and Duane and Debbie and Kym all had their mothers and even siblings along. As we grew older, our spouses and significant others and children always accompanied us when we were reunited. This is the first time that it is just the seven of us. Ever.

Sitting here, I am overwhelmed with memories. Being together on this plane feels like the first time we were put together during rehearsals in 1964, the first time we stood before the cameras, and the first time we journeyed across the Atlantic to a fairytale city surrounded by Alps.

It is as if we are in a time warp. We are the von Trapp family children again. And we are going home.

Something Good

As our plane descends toward Salzburg's airport, I feel a variety of emotions, from excitement to anticipation to exhaustion. We are back, and so much has happened in the years in between.

When we were making *The Sound of Music* upon the green hills below, I was so young. I had no idea how this would all turn out. I was excited to be making this movie, but couldn't visualize how all the little scenes we were filming would look. I didn't watch the daily rushes, and there was no such thing as video playback, and I actually worried sometimes that our film wouldn't be any good at all. I had no prior experience with which to gauge the quality of our work. I was unaware at the time that I was witnessing the birth of a masterpiece.

But the phenomenal success of the movie took everyone by surprise. Bob and Saul knew it was special, but even they couldn't foresee that *The Sound of Music* would break all the records. Until *Star Wars* and *Titanic, The Sound of Music* wasn't just the most successful musical film ever made; it was the most successful film, period, ultimately being named one of the three most popular films of all time by the People's Choice Awards. I have been told that a billion people have seen it - though there are times when I suspect that figure might be low.

I remember thinking at the fifth anniversary, when the studio brought the seven of us 'children' together for a reunion, "Well, this will be it." I honestly didn't expect people to continue to be so interested in the movie. Then the tenth anniversary came along, and it was still hugely successful, and then came the fifteenth. Finally, when the seven of us were in London to celebrate the twenty-fifth anniversary, I realized that people's love of *The Sound of Music* would go on forever and ever.

So many of the people responsible for making it all happen are no longer alive. Saul Chaplin, who added so much to the film, is gone, as are cast members Richard Haydn (Uncle Max), Peggy Wood (the Reverend Mother), Ben Wright (Herr Zeller), Gil Stuart (Franz the butler) and Norma Varden (Frau Schmidt). It's sad to me that they didn't live to see the impact of their efforts today. I doubt if any of them knew back in 1964 how wonderful the film they were making would be, and the magic effect it would have on audiences everywhere. For they created something good. Something really good. Fans from every corner of the globe have written to tell me they can't get enough of it.

Dear Charmian,

I am a dedicated patron of motion pictures, seeing some fifty or more a year, yet no film has had more of an impact on me than The Sound of Music. *I was fourteen when it premiered, and I actually attended in protest. But even before the intermission, I knew I had been transformed, and I remember later, not wanting it to end.*

I have seen many blockbusters and well-written movies, but I can honestly say not one of them had me meditating on what I had witnessed as deeply and as long as Sound of Music *did. How often does one see the same picture ten or more times? I suppose some people do, but not me. How often can one recall exactly what they were doing when a commercial for the re-release of a film is broadcast? I can. I was reading my local newspaper one morning in 1972, and I saw the ad announcing the re-release of* The Sound of Music *into theaters. I even remember exactly what it said: "The wait is over!"*

Over the years, untold numbers of fans have told me they think *The Sound of Music* is 'something good'. They have watched it more times than I can imagine, and have been touched by it in ways that I never fathomed possible.

I'm often amazed at the minute details they can recall about the first time they saw it. One man wrote me about the day he first saw the film as a boy in 1965. He could remember how the snow was falling that day, "one of those lovely snowfalls where the wind swirls the flakes around, and they land in a powder rather than packing down." That he is able to remember what the weather was like thirty-five years ago on a day when he watched a movie astounds me. But he is not alone.

I first saw The Sound of Music *at the Uptown Theater in Utica, New York when it first opened. My mom took my best friend and me on a Friday night. Janie and I were six, and there was a snow storm that day and my dad drove us to the theater in his old Scout pickup. There was a line around the block, but Dad had bought our tickets days ahead.*

The Uptown was an old regal movie house with a balcony and red velvet seats and ushers - and the biggest screen I had ever seen. Here we were, two little girls dressed to the nines, with hot buttered popcorn and lime soda and Raisinettes and that wonderful, wonderful movie and score.

I fell in love with The Sound of Music *that night. Today, it remains my all time favorite move, and the only one I own on video. And to this day, I can still drive by that old theater on a snowy evening and see those two little wide-eyed girls on our first big night out. Thanks for the memory...*

Such memories live in people's hearts, all over the world.

I was born in England and The Sound of Music *was the first "real" movie that I ever saw. To this day, I remember fondly getting dressed up, including wearing my shiny black patent leather shoes and going to the main cinema in London. The balcony and the huge curtains just added to the grandeur of the occasion.*

Of course, people not only have strong visual memories of the first time they saw it, but also of subsequent viewings.

I attended the premiere of The Sound of Music's *25ᵗʰ Anniversary re-release at the Century Plaza Theater. I started crying at the very first scene and didn't stop the whole movie... it was great!*

The entire audience sang along with every song and gave a big ovation after every song ended. It was so beautiful to see it on the big screen again. I just wanted to share the memory...

They remember when it first aired on television. The anger of fans to scenes being cut down for network television is universal, as the following letter demonstrates.

Like most of America, I grew up with The Sound of Music. *I was ten-years-old the first time I saw the movie...and ten-years-old the second time I saw it...and the third time and the fourth. In those days, I could get a Saturday matinee ticket and stay through two showings of the film. I did this several times when the film first came out, and again when the film was re-released a few years later. I memorized the dialogue, and of course bought the soundtrack album when it first came out on vinyl (I still have it!)*

I was both thrilled and outraged when the film was finally on television: thrilled because it was my favorite movie, and outraged when portions of the dialogue and songs were edited to make room for commercials. Having memorized the film, I was acutely aware of the gaping holes omitted from the original. In my mind, editing the movie for commercial air time was tantamount to vandalism of a masterpiece. It was the same as tampering with the Mona Lisa (or should I say Mona Liesl?!) Needless to say, The Sound of Music *was the first video I ever bought. Never again did I have to growl about the film being edited for television. All of the dialogue and all of the songs were at last restored in their entirety.*

For many younger fans of the film, their first introduction to the movie was not on the big screen, but on the small one.

Dear Charmian,

I was forced to watch The Sound of Music *for the first time when I was 7. I begged my mom to bring me home a cartoon from the video store and instead she brought* The Sound of Music. *I was so mad at my mother - until she put in the first tape. I fell in love with the movie, and have been ever since...*

The memories that people have of the film and the music are lifelong, spanning every era of their lives and every generation of their families.

"Climb Ev'ry Mountain" has been my theme song for my life since 1965. I had it sung at my wedding. My youngest daughter learned every line and song by the time she was eight. At her request, I made her a dress for a special banquet that was just like 'Liesl's', with a full skirt, but sleeves like the blue one Maria wore when the Captain first sang Edelweiss. My daughter had always dreamed of having a wedding veil like Maria's, a dream that was fulfilled last year.

The Sound of Music *has been a deep and lasting positive influence in my life and that of my children. I don't know any other movie that has so influenced people, affected their lives, and crossed generations and tied them together, than this movie. Thank you for being such a wonderful part of my youth and my life...*

Peggy Wood, who played the Reverend Mother, would be very happy to hear this woman's words. I hope Peggy knows, wherever she is, how much people love "Climb Ev'ry Mountain".

It's wonderful how many people have used "Maria's" wedding march in their own ceremonies. It's such a beautiful piece of music. I wish I'd thought of it myself!

The Sound of Music *was the first movie my mom took me to see in downtown Chicago in 1964. I had the wedding march from the movie in my wedding in 1983, and the movie now has become one of my daughter's favorites!*

The film's influence upon people is potent and the Trapp family's story is, for many, their fantasy of a perfect life.

I am one of eight children. We were in deep financial trouble in 1967 when my mother packed us in the station wagon to see The Sound of Music *at a drive-in outside Albuquerque.*

I was mesmerized. I remember watching through the grape soda one of the other kids sitting on the roof of the car had poured over the windshield. The idea that there was such a place, such a situation! Seven children with money, running around the gorgeous Austrian countryside, singing and dancing in the sunshine. I wanted to go there!

I asked my mother how those kids got into that movie. She didn't know. But I became determined to get there. Get into movies. Live a life like those children. And I did, to an extent. I studied. Got a college degree in acting. Moved to L.A. I've had a nice acting career.

But I've always thought, it will never be like THEIR lives. Like those kids. The Sound of Music *was so perfect...*

The Sound of Music <u>is</u> perfect, but our lives aren't. The film gives people something to strive for, to come close to, but I hope no one ever measures their lives against it. Even all of us who were lucky enough to have been a part of the film have suffered and struggled in life. Still, I think it's lovely that this young man chose to reach for such a high ideal as the family life and values of the von Trapps.

Parents have told me how they have scrimped and saved to be able to take their children to see this one film.

In 1965, we cashed in our pennies to be able to see The Sound of Music *as a family with our daughter, then five, and our son, then just three-and-a-half. To us, it was the best money ever spent on a family outing...*

I've never had anyone tell me that they wished they'd saved their money. Their letters show me how the movie and the music are more than entertainment for them: it is food for their souls.

When the video first came out, it cost anywhere from $79 to $100? I wanted the video so badly. I also knew that would be the only video I'd ever want to own. I didn't even have a VCR. But I saved up for the video, and then got a VCR, and only owned the two!

All I can say is, if someone has a VCR and only owns one video, *The Sound of Music* is the one to have, for it has the ability to make them happy.

When I graduated from high school, I took the money I had received and didn't save for college or to buy something I didn't need. I bought this movie because I needed it! It is awesome!

As a mother, I don't know if I totally approve (a college education is important!). But as 'Liesl', I'm honored that the film is so meaningful to people, and I love that college students today enjoy the film.

I am nineteen and my suitemates in college and I just watched The Sound of Music. *We talked about how it was our favorite movie of all time and how when we were little, we all wanted to be Liesl. Who wouldn't!*

There is one person who loved the film and the story so much, she created her own version.

As a teen in the mid-1970's, I decided to do a film (home movie style). Perhaps it is the first remake of The Sound of Music. *I was seventeen and I rounded up all* the kids from my neighborhood who thought this would be a lot of fun. Our youngest cast member was five (she played Gretl) and I can still remember how much fun she had learning all her lines.

We found clothes at yard sales and I made costumes to look as close to the originals as possible. We even made puppets for the puppet show scene.

Most of the scenes were filmed in the Richmond area, but we did take the whole cast and crew to the mountains of Virginia for a whole weekend to film the picnic scene and other outdoor scenes from "Do-Re-Me". It was not as beautiful as Salzburg, but it was close to home!

I think the parents had as much fun as the kids. It took us several years to complete our project (it started out just to be a couple of scenes, but everyone had so much fun with it, we kept adding new scenes, filming mainly during school breaks and summer vacation.) By then I was in college and used the film for a film-making class.

The summer of 1976, my parents took my sister (who played Liesl) and I to Austria and I got a chance to shoot some real footage for my movie. Unfortunately, we couldn't take any of the other kids with us. We filmed outside the Abbey and at the same house that was used for the front of the von Trapp villa when Maria 'arrives'. My dad got permission to be inside the door (dressed as the butler) and answered the door for that scene. We were also lucky enough to use the other home that was used as the back of the villa and the terrace and lake are just as beautiful as they are in the movie.

As the kids grew taller I realized that we had to finish up our project. Some of the kids were even changing their hairstyles so it was hard to film.

My best memory of the whole experience is of how we took the glimmer of an idea and, with a lot of fun and team work, turned it into a project we were all proud of. These kids were no longer just my neighbors - they became family. To this day, my mom still thinks she has seven kids!

People have been asking for years if there will ever be a remake of *The Sound of Music*. Little did I know, it's already been done. As I read this letter, I wanted to move into this woman's neighborhood. What fun! If imitation is the highest form of flattery, then the fact that someone spent three years trying to duplicate what we did in *The Sound of Music* suggests we should all be very flattered. Of course, not everyone needs to remake the film. Some people can literally replay the original in their mind.

Ever since I was about twelve, when people ask me if I have any hidden talents, I tell them I can recite The Sound of Music *in its entirety - which is true. It's something I love being known for.*

I'm very involved in my church and pretty much known throughout the Archdiocese of Boston for my ability to recite my favorite movie. When I get into an argument with someone, I stop and say lines from the film until the person has nothing more to say because I can keep going the whole movie. And when I can't fall asleep at night, I recite the movie to myself and watch it in my head.

Some people *do* watch it more frequently than I think I could.

I just wanted to tell you that since I was 3 years old (I'm now 38) The Sound of Music *has been my all time favorite. You can't imagine how my life has evolved around this film, how many different copies of the album I have owned. I even made my family postpone a fishing trip when I was 7 because it was playing for the weekend at our local theater. I believe I've seen this film over 600 times...*

Though I don't think I could watch *The Sound of Music* that many times, I love the fact that the film means so much to this young man, and I'm glad that he was able to see *The Sound of Music* as a seven-year-old rather than kill some poor fish.

With the advent of the VCR, children have grown up watching this film as much as they want - which is often.

My mother used to beg my sister and I to choose another video. "Please?" she would say, "Please! What about some nice cartoons?" But no, it was always The Sound of Music, *almost every weekend. It's not that my mum didn't like the film or the music. It's just that we would watch the film and rewind it and watch it again and love it even more, and she got a bit sick of it.*

My sister and I would speak along with the von Trapp children and go with Maria on her journey as she falls in love with the Captain. We would stand there with our hands clasped in front of us and sing "So Long, Farewell." We knew every moment of The Sound of Music *and adored every second, and nothing could quell our tireless love of the songs and the sweetness of the film that embedded itself into our childhood, and hence, into our memories...*

Children watch it over and over to play out childhood fantasies of being a part of that family, and adults watch it over and over to lift their spirits. Many have found the themes and messages in the film help them get through dreary days.

I have been a fan of The Sound of Music *since I saw it in a theater at the age of 4 (I am now 28 and a teacher). I watch it often. It is the perfect accompaniment to grading papers and bad mood days. I just watched the film again the other day and found myself tearing up throughout it. I really believe that film holds many spiritual messages in it and that it meant for our society to remind us that love does prevail - and we are here to help one another...*

I couldn't agree more. Some even feel the film could be a deterrent for those disenfranchised among us.

I have a theory that if every bum, stiff, stealer, robber and potential bad guy or gal would just take a few hours to watch The Sound of Music, *we'd have a lot less crime on our streets...*

People's love for the film never seems to diminish. And sometimes the ways in which their lives have become intertwined with the film touches me to the core.

When I was thirteen, I was rewarded a VHS tape of The Sound of Music *for having excellent grades in school. I'd never seen the movie before, and couldn't for the life of me figure out why my beloved mother would buy it. Finally, after much convincing, we sat down together and watched it. I immediately fell in love with the film.*

But most important to me is my mother's love for the movie. She was such a wonderful part of my life. She died in 1985, when I was seventeen, just four years after introducing me to the film.

When my mother died, my best friend and I watched the movie together, and I cried at the end. I could almost hear my mother's voice telling me to "Climb Ev'ry Mountain."

I'm thirty-two now, and you've always seemed like a big sister to me. Thank you for such a wonderful and touching film.

People ask me why this film endures. "What makes it so good?" I don't think there is any one reason. There's no 'best part' of the film, it's all seamlessly perfect. If you took away any one of the main components, it wouldn't be the masterpiece that it is. The melodies, the lyrics, the natural beauty of the landscape, the people in front of the cameras and the people behind the cameras, all combine to make something uniquely special.

What if Julie Andrews hadn't been in the film? What if the locales had been shot on a soundstage rather than on location in Salzburg? What if Ernie Lehman hadn't written it or Bob Wise hadn't directed it or composers other than Rodgers and Hammerstein had written the music?

The Sound of Music is a magic convergence of many things, and it's success rests upon so many people. Six of them are sitting beside me right now as the wheels of our plane touch down on the runway of the Salzburg Airport, and I know they'd agree with me: there isn't a single person or thing that you can point to and say, "This is why it worked." *The Sound of Music* just does. Everyone involved in the production, from the top to the bottom, worked hard to make something good.

They succeeded.

On the Road with Liesl

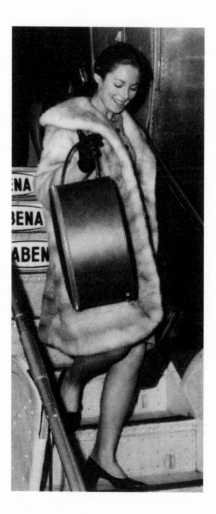

Our Austrian Airlines jet rolls to a stop on the runway, and when the door is opened, there are limos on the tarmac waiting for us. In a private lounge within the airport, we are greeted by a number of Austrian dignitaries. The lounge is beautiful, like an 18th century Austrian palace, and there are silver flutes of champagne and Mozart chocolates and an alderman from Salzburg who formally welcomes us to the country.

We are treated like visiting royalty. I didn't expect this kind of treatment. We are simply seven actors, returning to the site of a film location thirty-six years after the fact to make a documentary, yet the people of Salzburg make us feel like treasured icons from the instant we set foot on Austrian soil.

We never go through customs. After the brief reception, we find our bags have already been loaded into the limos, and we are whisked away to our hotel. As we approach the city, I am struck by how unchanged everything is. Salzburg looks exactly as it did in when we made the movie, even better. All the buildings are pristine and gleaming, and I feel an eerie deja vu as we drive through the city streets. I remember well the day we arrived here in April of 1964, and how it felt to be young and free in this fairytale city, with no cares, no worries. I feel that way again, right now.

At the hotel, we meet our British producer, Judith Holder, and her crew. There are seven of them and seven of us: perfect symmetry. Though we've only spoken to Judith by phone, there are hugs and kisses all around before we sit down at a long, long table for dinner.

Everyone is talking non-stop, but as I glance around the table, I can see that excitement is giving way to exhaustion. It will be an early evening for many of us, certainly for me. Traveling can take the wind out of one's sails. I know this all too well.

Back when the film was initially released, I traveled the world for

Twentieth Century Fox, appearing at film premieres for *The Sound of Music* in Europe and South America and Asia and the Carribean. I loved it. My life's goal before I was chosen to play Liesl had been to save up enough money to travel to Europe. Ironically, *The Sound of Music* became my passport to see the world.

I have loved being the film's 'ambassador', and have always felt very proud and fortunate to be affiliated with it, and enjoyed the opportunity to represent it. So, when my book was released in 2000, and I was back on the road again across North America, I should have felt I was on very familiar turf. But launching my book was very different than representing the film. This wasn't a movie about someone else's life, this was *my* story. This was personal. So, although I had never felt nervous being on the road with the film, I was petrified as I set off for New York for the debut of Forever Liesl.

In a way, it was the first moment I truly stepped into the von Trapps' shoes. They had been living with their story in the public arena for half a century. Now, I was joining them. I spent days worrying as the launch date approached.

The Today Show was first. I sat in the Green Room (which wasn't green at all) anxiously waiting my turn to go on, but when my name was called, my fears were immediately dispelled by Katie Couric. She was incredibly nice and seemed so genuinely interested in the book that I quickly felt right at home. Within a few moments, she had me laughing, and by the end of the interview, I was completely at ease.

Like so many people I would encounter over the coming weeks and months, she was a true fan of the film. ("Every time I watch it," she said, "and believe me, I've seen it plenty, and I'm always moved.") When the interview ended, we chatted about her two daughters while the studio crew and newscaster Ann Curry serenaded us with songs from *The Sound of Music*. Forever Liesl was officially launched.

That evening I attended my first book signing at the Lincoln Triangle, and a tradition was born. Two little girls in line asked me if I would sing them a song from the film, so I pulled them close and sang, "I am sixteen, going on seventeen..." They loved it, grinning from ear to ear, singing softly along with me, and when I looked up, I realized that the entire bookstore had grown quiet, listening to us. In almost every city I visited after that, someone in the crowd would ask me to sing. After thirty-five years, I was Liesl again.

One of the most enjoyable interviews I've ever done happened next with Scott Simon on NPR in Washington, DC. He was a big fan of "Liesl", yet his enthusiasm for the film was balanced with his intelligence, so he didn't ask the standard questions I generally get asked. He kept me on my toes, and apparently, I kept him on his, too, because right in the middle of our interview, he got so flustered he fumbled and dropped his pencil, and later confessed that in all the years he's been doing interviews, he'd never done that before. For me, a rookie author, this was a high compliment!

Next, the book tour took me to Baltimore where I dined with Agathe, the oldest surviving member of the original seven von Trapp children. Like the other members of her family, Agathe is a remarkable human being, and it's extremely special for me when I'm able to spend time with her. I was so honored when, after dinner, she accompanied me to the book store and sat for an hour, signing books right alongside me.

My "Sound of Music" family helped me all along the way. When the tour took me to Minnesota, the enormous crowd that turned out was in for a surprise. Debbie, (Marta in the film), joined me, and later, like Agathe, she sat beside me and signed books for the long line of fans. The next day, my 'little sister' took me snowmobiling on the frozen lake near her house. I'd never been snowmobiling before, and I could hear the ice pinging which made it all the more exciting. It was so fun being with

Debbie, and I'm so proud of what she's accomplished with her business career and her four beautiful daughters.

It was on to Seattle where I was reunited with yet another member of our "Sound of Music" family: Duane Chase (Kurt). Over lunch, he and I were able to catch up on all that had happened since I'd seen him last. His wife, Petra, who happens to be Austrian (and whose middle name is Maria!), told me she'd read the book and loved it, and it meant a great deal to me to know that a 'member of the family' appreciated it.

Upon my return home, I would receive a letter from another member of "the family" who'd also read the book: Julie Andrews.

I just returned home to find a copy of your book "Forever Liesl" waiting for me on my desk...

Browsing through it brought back so many happy memories and reminded me of some details that I had actually forgotten. I am thrilled to have it. It's probably safe to say that that amazing movie affected all our *lives. I am grateful that I was able to be a part of it and so pleased that you have captured those memorable days on paper...*

Julie and I don't see each other often, but we'll always be connected because of this one film, and that's a nice feeling. And she's absolutely right: *The Sound of Music* did change all our lives.

When my tour ended in San Francisco, over three thousand miles from where it had begun, attending the signing was a little four-year-old girl. Unlike the little girls who attended my first signing in New York, she didn't ask me to sing to her. She raised her hand, announcing, "I've seen *The Sound of Music* a hundred million times."

"You have?"

"Yes. And I know your song."

"You mean 'Sixteen Going on Seventeen'?"

She nodded and then proceeded to sing the entire song, and it was wonderfully ironic to me that I had begun the tour singing to children and ended it by being serenaded by a child.

Dear Charmy,

Why didn't you come to Atlanta?

When will you be touring in Florida?

Please come to Salt Lake City so we can meet you!

Are you ever coming to England?

After the publisher's tour ended I heard from people the world over asking me to come everywhere from Alaska to Maine and Argentina to Australia, so I went out on my own, whenever I could afford to. My co-author said, "You should go to Worcester, Massachusetts." She'd lived there and claimed the city had the best bookstore in the United States.

I was skeptical as she drove me from New York to Massachusetts, but when we arrived at Tatnuck Booksellers, I was overwhelmed by the enormous crowd awaiting us. And she was right: the bookstore *was* fabulous.

But before I answered any questions or signed any books, the first order of business was that Maria von Trapp was waiting for me on the store's telephone. Unbeknownst to me, Maria, in her mid-eighties, had heard I was coming to Massachusetts and had planned to drive all the way from her home in Vermont to surprise me. Her travel arrangements had fallen through, but I was so touched that she had even considered the four hundred mile trek.

Returning to New York, I had an unexpected treat. Charlie Prince (the son of Hal Prince and grandson of Saul Chaplin) invited me to see a play he was music director for on Broadway, and afterwards, he took me backstage to see one of the stars of the show: Marni Nixon. Marni had played Sister Sophia in *The Sound of Music* (and had provided the singing voice for Audrey Hepburn in *My Fair Lady* and Natalie Wood in *West Side Story*). She jumped up to gave me a big hug and it felt like a homecoming right there in her dressing room. Our *Sound of Music* family is everywhere.

Dear Charmian Carr,
When are you coming to Canada?

There are so many parts of the world I haven't been able to visit yet, but there is one place in particular that I wanted to be sure to get to: Canada. My father is a Canadian, and it's where my older sister Sharon was born, so I've always felt that I, too, have roots there. When an opportunity arose for me to go to Toronto, I jumped at the chance.

A book signing was set up on very short notice, and when I arrived, I was told it was going to be at a Walmart, not in Toronto, but in Mississauga. My initial thought was that not many people would go to a department store in a suburb for a book signing. I couldn't have been more wrong.

As the publisher's rep drove into the parking lot, I gasped. A long line of people stretched around the store. I thought, they couldn't all be here for the book. But they were.

Nearly four hundred people had been waiting for two hours. I was on a very tight schedule, and the book rep advised me that everyone in line had already been told that I wouldn't talk or answer questions, that I would only sign books. But I looked at that long, patient, line and said, "They came all this way. I'm not going to disappoint them." So I answered a million questions and then sat down and began to meet them, one by one. There was one woman who I'll never forget. She was from

India, and when she reached the head of the line, she began to cry and couldn't stop. She was shaking, and I held her hand while she told me how much she loved the film and how she couldn't believe she was meeting me. I almost began to cry with her.

An hour passed, and then another, and the line never seemed to get any shorter. The book rep said it was time to leave or I'd miss my flight. I shook my head. There were still a hundred people waiting.

Dear Charmian,

My wife and I met you in Mississauga, Ontario, Canada on Friday. We were the last few fans in the lineup waiting to greet you and it was well worth the long wait to have met "Liesl" in person after watching the movie back in the sixties and then sharing it with our three children time and again while they were growing up.

Thank you...

I missed my plane to New York and didn't get out until the next day, but it meant so much to me that all those people had come.

I was going camping the day you came to Mississauga, and I talked my friend into driving me the thirty plus miles to meet you. Our detour to meet you was well worth arriving at the campground hours late.

What does one say when they are in front of someone who has dominated their life? I had no idea what to say to you. I do remember telling you that I had spent my lunch hour that day looking for plastic spiders to put in a jar to bring you, but couldn't find any. Thank you for coming. I will always remember kissing "Liesl" on the cheek...

I'll always remember their reception, their enthusiasm, and I will return to Canada again, someday.

Over the years, when people have asked me about the film, I tend to get asked very similar questions. What's Julie Andrews like? What was it like filming specific moments? What are my favorite scenes and songs? But while touring with the book, I've been asked some new questions.

One little boy boldly asked, "Are you rich?" and when I stopped laughing I could tell him that I was certainly rich in friends.

When I was asked when I'd do another book, I'd ask for suggestions of what to call it. Fans came up with some very creative titles. "Forever and Ever Liesl." "Forever Lethal." "Liesl Weapon." And my favorite, "Liesl: The Dark Side."

In Santa Fe, New Mexico, I got asked a question I had no idea how to answer: "What do you want on your tombstone?"

I'd never thought about it and stood there with my mind blank trying to think of what to say when a woman in the audience helped me out. "How about 'no longer sixteen going on seventeen.'"

Everyone roared, and I said that sounded just perfect. Who knows, maybe I'll use it.

I certainly didn't feel sixteen-going-on-seventeen while I was doing all this traveling. Like my celluloid siblings on our first night back in Austria, living out of a suitcase left me feeling exhausted at times. And astounded.

I would never have guessed back in 1965 when I began touring with the film that I would still be out, meeting with fans who the film has touched, in the new millennium.

Being on the road with <u>Forever Liesl</u> has defined for me the word 'forever'. *The Sound of Music,* and the special joy it brings to people's lives, will never die.

The Liesl Club

Today is the first day of filming our documentary. It's a crisp autumn day and I wake early and spend a few moments gazing out my hotel window at the tile roofs and mountain cliffs of Salzburg. A wave of old feelings wells up inside. I am Liesl and I am in Salzburg once again.

In 1964, I was twenty-one and it was intoxicating to be young and free in this fairytale city, thousands of miles from home. That sense of freedom overtakes me again, three and a half decades later. I want to go out and play, but there is work to be done, a film to be made, and that reminds me of my days long ago in Salzburg when, during my off-time while making *The Sound of Music,* I worked on a documentary called *Salzburg: Sight and Sound.* Working on both films at the same time didn't leave me much free time for sightseeing or play, and I smile, thinking about the day's schedule ahead. This trip really *is* reliving the past.

I was on the brink of adulthood back then, and like Liesl, was in many ways innocent and naive. The three months in Salzburg transformed me. For the first time in my life, I felt like a grown up, and began to appreciate not only the freedom of adulthood, but the responsibility that went with it. Being "Liesl" changed me.

Though Liesl is a fictional character, to this day I am identified as her. People still stop me in the street, in the grocery store, even though I'm in my late fifties. "Are you Liesl?" I guess it's the blue eyes and the dimples and the fact that people have seen the film so many times that my face and voice seem familiar to them.

Of course, nowadays they often recognize me without making the connection, stopping me and wondering if we might have known each other in high school or in college, and when I tell them it's probably *The Sound of Music* they shout, "Oh my god! You're Liesl!"

The name alone is distinctive and immediately makes people think of the film. In fact, being "Liesl" has prompted me to create The Liesl Club.

This organization was inspired by many letters similar to this one.

My name is Liesl; I was named after your character in the movie. The first thing anyone ever says to me is, "Liesl? Oh, like in The Sound of Music?*"*

I have spent the better part of my life explaining the proper spelling and pronunciation to people.

I can relate. I couldn't pronounce the name myself when I first saw it in the script. I thought it was pronounced Lysol. Some parents try to compensate for these pronunciation issues right from the start.

My daughter, Leizl, was named after your role in The Sound of Music. *We changed the spelling for the 'Texas accents' to pronounce it right! She loves her name, and is always asked where she got it...*

What wise parents to provide phonetic spelling before sending their children off to school! It's much better than being called Lysol or Lissel or Lie-zell. But no matter how you spell it or say it, there are thousands of girls and women out there who are members of this very select club. To belong is simple: you just need to be named Liesl. Everywhere I go, I meet members.

When I was in Denver on my book tour, there were two young women standing next to each other in line at a book store. They didn't know each other, but when the first one handed me her book, and said, "My name is Liesl," the young woman behind her blurted out, "You're kidding! My name is Liesl, too!" The two of them did a double take and all three of us burst out laughing. I've always felt a special bond with young women like these who have been named for Liesl von Trapp.

My parents instilled the movie lover in me when they chose my name: Liesl. When The Sound of Music *was shown on television, I would be glued to the screen, waiting for my name to appear, and then I'd recite your lines along with you on the screen. The last time I saw the film on TV was on the eve of my sixteenth birthday. Everyone at school the next day could not help but serenade me with "I am Sixteen, Going on Seventeen". That is a day I will never forget...*

I doubt that *Music's* playwrights, Lindsay and Crouse, knew that they were naming an entire generation of girls when they named the oldest von Trapp "Liesl" instead of Rupert, but that's exactly what they did.

Our daughter, Liesl, was named after your character in The Sound of Music. *One of the questions she is always asked is how she got her name...*

It feels pretty good to have all these girls named after Liesl. It is such a pretty name, and it's wonderful to hear how fond people are of the character, and how that love is passed from one generation to the next.

I have always been very proud of my name for being so unique and the knowledge of where it came from. I thank my mother for that, for falling in love with The Sound of Music. *She named me after your character when I was born in 1966, and I am now a mother of two girls of my own, and as my mother did, I'm sharing with them my love for the movie...*

Actually, you don't have to be named Liesl to be a member of the club. There is a whole subset of other women and girls who are automatically inducted: all the actresses who have played Liesl on stage.

You and I share a common bond. My sophomore year in high school, I was blessed with the character role of ... you got it... Liesl. From the very first rehearsal to the tear-filled last performance, I was consumed with "Liesl". Her character and the person I am are so similar that being her was almost like being me, in costume.

I hope that somehow you get this letter, and that you know there is a 16-going-on-17 year old girl in Colorado who admires you and feels totally connected to you...

We *are* connected, because in a way, we became the same person for a while on stage when we immersed ourselves in the role of the oldest von Trapp. This is a bond I share with hundreds, if not thousands of teenage girls and young women who have played Liesl.

I have wanted to be a stage actress since I can remember, and a childhood dream of mine was to someday play Liesl. This summer, my dream come true. I, too, am - if only temporarily - Liesl. In less than three weeks, I will tell the audience at the Connecticut community theater where I am performing that I am "sixteen going on seventeen"...

My mother used to sing "My Favorite Things" to me as a lullaby when I was very little, and before long I knew all the words to every song on the "Music" soundtrack. I don't remember the first time I saw the movie, but I used to watch it when I was home sick from school, and it always cheered me up. Initially, when I was cast as Liesl, I was resolved not to watch the film again before the show. Last week, however, I was having some trouble getting into character, and I decided to watch the movie again, this time from an actor's angle. I did, and was very happy afterwards that I chose to do so. It brought back all the memories of when I used to watch it as a little kid, and it helped me to better understand who the character of Liesl truly is.

I was quite sure when we started rehearsing back in May that I would soon grow tired of singing "I am sixteen going on seventeen" over an over. But I haven't yet... and I doubt I ever will.

I am still singing "Sixteen" to this day, and I have never ever tired of the song. Rodgers and Hammerstein were geniuses.

The role of Liesl has, whether I've been aware of it or not, made me a part of people's lives.

My twelve year old daughter played Liesl in a summer theater production of The Sound of Music. *For the six weeks prior to the performances we watched the movie, sometimes twice, daily. You were like part of the family!*

For some girls it is a childhood dream to play Liesl.

From the time my sister and I had enough of an attention span to sit in front of a movie, we watched The Sound of Music *compulsively. We used to randomly run through the house with pillowcases on our heads (we were being "nuns") and could reenact most of the movie with almost the original choreography (save a few scraped knees from attempting to leap from bench to bench). As little girls, we never quite aspired to be Maria; I guess that whole nun thing was never very appealing, and besides, who wanted to carry the whole movie anyway. So Liesl it was.*

I'm a brunette and my sister is a blond, so, despite the fact that I always had a good half foot on her, I simply HAD to be Liesl. Last summer, I turned 16, which I found extraordinarily pressing because I was quickly outgrowing all of the parts. Imagine my delight and surprise when it was announced that my school would be performing The Sound of Music. *Naturally, I knew what part I wanted - as did three-quarters of the girls who tried out. Luckily, I was cast, and your interpretation of the role will always be an inspiration to me...*

For one young woman, playing Liesl provided a way of reconnecting with her parents.

I remember vividly the night that my mother took my brother and me to see The Sound of Music *when it was first released. I fell in love with the story, the scenery, and the characters. I know life is not a fairy tale existence, but the story the film tells is of hope and perseverance, something I pray I have in my life. When I was in college, I, too, played Liesl. In many ways, the play and the role changed my life.*

Doing the play was important to me for several reasons, but the most important one is that my parents came to see me in The Sound of Music. *This was after a period of time when they did not see my work, and they have since become faithful attenders and supporters of me on the stage.*

There is yet another subset to the Liesl Club: all the young women who have been saddled with my real name, Charmian, because of *The Sound of Music.* If I mispronounced Liesl at first, it was nothing compared to the mispronunciations I have heard for Charmian. Generally, my name ends up sounding like a dish one would order in a Chinese restaurant. Char-maine. Or Chair-man. Or Char-Mine. Few people give it the 'sh' sound on the first try. It takes practice to get it right. Shar-mee-in. Because of *The Sound of Music,* I have inadvertently passed on this burden to others.

I have followed your career for as long as I can remember because it is because of you that I am who I am. My name is Charmian. Yes, my mother picked the name because of you and your appearance in The Sound of Music. *She believed it was a beautiful name and on her first date with my father, she told him she would someday have a daughter named Charmian.*

It's always been very hard to introduce myself to others. I often get called Charmaine or Charmin' after the toilet paper... and people often have trouble with the 'sh' sound instead of the hard 'c'. But if someone says it right, it really is the most beautiful name. When an article appeared about you in People Magazine, *I cut it out to show all my friends - this was where I got my weird name!*

The young sons of one of my friends always used to say "Don't squeeze the Charmin'" whenever I came over to their house, so I can totally relate. All I can say to all of those Charmian's out there everywhere is, I'm so very sorry. But I agree with the woman above: when it's said correctly, Charmian *is* a beautiful name.

There is one last subset in the Liesl Club: all those young girls who are 16-going-on-17. For them, the character and the song signify first love and approaching womanhood. I think most sixteen and seventeen-year-old's can relate to the characters of Liesl and Rolf because they are experiencing their own first loves.

I was really looking forward to my birthday because it meant that I would be the same age as Liesl. Right now, I really am sixteen going on seventeen, and it is really exciting. Ever since I was five, I wished I was sixteen. I feel a bond with you, as if you were a long lost relative.

It is a wonderful thing to be a grandmother and still be identified as a character who signifies youth and young love. That teenagers feel a bond with me is something I treasure. Some young people who write me are quite perceptive about how fleeting their youth can be.

The Sound of Music has been a part of my life since before I could talk. Last year, when I turned sixteen, I sang "Sixteen Going on Seventeen" all over my house until suddenly I realized: I was the same age as the oldest von Trapp.

The film has shaped my life in many ways, so when I was given an assignment in a class to give a speech about one of my most treasured objects, I brought in our old worn-out copy of The Sound of Music *video. And in an English class, I had to read a book outside our regular list and then present it to the class. I did your memoir and, dressed as Liesl, turned what was supposed to be a five minute presentation into a twenty-five minute soliloquy.*

On Halloween this year, three weeks before I turned seventeen, I wore the same costume to school, dancing as Liesl through the halls to "Sixteen Going on Seventeen". There are still some underclassmen who just refer to me as Liesl...

I love to hear such stories, and to envision how the character has given many teens someone they can identify with. I like knowing that "Liesl" has helped people. To be honest, there was a period in my life when I felt "Liesl" was a burden. In the first few years after the film came out, I felt uncertain whether I was being invited and included because I was Charmian - or because I was Liesl. Some people wanted to be my friend simply because I'd been in *The Sound of Music* and that bothered me. I actually resented the character for a while. I think all of us who were involved with the film, particularly the children, struggled with these identity issues.

But, despite this, there was never a moment when I regretted my involvement in the film. I'll always feel blessed to have been a part of it. And, more than anyone else in my life, the fans of the film are the ones who encouraged me to see the gift I'd been given by Liesl.

My mother loved the movie so much, she named me Liesl after you. Every year we would watch The Sound of Music *when it was on TV and it always made me feel special that I was named after a character from such a wonderful movie.*

My mother passed away when I was 12. But whenever I start to miss her, I just pop in the video and it always seems to make me feel better. I know it sounds silly, but I guess it makes me feel connected to her through my name...

It doesn't sound silly at all. I'm grateful and honored that the film has the ability to make people feel better when they are sad. That the name Liesl can also make a young woman feel more connected to her lost mother simply overwhelms me.

My membership in The Liesl Club is something I cherish. There are thousands of us, if not millions. To join, all you need is to be sixteen-going-on-seventeen at heart. That's something I intend to be, forever.

Bachelor Dandies

This evening here in Salzburg, after a day spent working non-stop on the documentary, the seven of us sit down to an elegant table and laugh and reminisce late into the night. Back in 1964, "Liesl" might not have gotten to stay and taste her first champagne, but *I* did. I was housed at the same hotel as many of the other adults, and spent many late nights and early mornings in the lobby of the Bristol Hotel, listening to Christopher Plummer play the piano, and learning to appreciate fine wine. So this evening, I have to laugh at how times have changed. Not only is Liesl imbibing on champagne, so are Friedrich and Louisa and Kurt and Brigitta and Marta and even little Gretl. I wish Chris Plummer were here with us. He would enjoy this revelry we "children" share here in Salzburg as adults, and he would now have a thing or two he could teach his "family."

I so enjoyed the times spent in Salzburg with Chris. Hysterically funny and purposely irreverent, he tried hard to keep all of us from taking ourselves too seriously. Only thirteen years separated us in age, and it was fun for me to flirt with him, and to be included with the other adults in his late night concerts. It would be a hoot to have him here now for the other 'kids' to be exposed to his wicked sense of fun.

I loved working with Chris, but have seen him only rarely since the filming ended. Of all the people I met while making *The Sound of Music*, there's one person I've remained truly close to all these years: Nicholas Hammond. He was a boy, just thirteen-going-on-fourteen, when I first met him, and I've been privileged to know him my entire adult life.

I remember when he went off to college thinking, "My goodness, Nicky's at Princeton. This is really something!" But it wasn't until his wedding day that I saw him as he was: all grown up, a man. I was so proud of him that day. He had come a long way from when we danced together on a sound stage in Los Angeles as brother and sister.

Through the years, he's always been there for me, and I hope I've always been there for him. In the most difficult periods of my life, he's one of the people who's never left my side, and who's always able to set things right. I wrote about the special relationship we share in <u>Forever Liesl</u>, and it prompted a few letters like the one below.

Dear Charmy,

Why don't you marry Nicky?

I think it's a lovely idea. At my age, I've decided it might be more sensible to be with someone *younger* and wiser, and at eight years my junior, Nicky would be the ideal match. And our relationship is perfect. He's my best friend. There's just one hitch: he hasn't asked me.

But over the years, a lot of other young men and boys (and some not-so-young ones, too) have written me notes, professing deep feelings for Liesl. These 'bachelor dandies' have brightened my life with their wit, with their endearing youthful optimism, and with their kind words.

One such fan, a sailor aboard a ship in the Indian Ocean, wrote me a letter back in 1965, in which he expressed how he felt *The Sound of Music* carried a universal message, opening people's eyes to the potential courage and goodness in all mankind. He went on to tell me a story.

His brother, who was also a sailor, had dropped a message in a bottle into the sea off Madagascar. The message said that if a girl should find the bottle, he'd love for her to write him and tell him where she found it. The bottle ended up washing ashore on a beach only twenty miles from his brother's home, and was found by a pretty girl, and a romance developed between them.

This inspired the young sailor to write to me. He thought it unlikely that if he dropped a message in a bottle into the Indian Ocean that the bottle would find it's way to a California beach for me to find, so he was using the conventional method of an addressed and stamped envelope. He wrote me about the beauty of the sea and how the moon made the spray off the bow glitter at night like the light of a thousand diamonds. He told me how a sailor feels to be alone amid such beauty, and that invariably, most sailors think of a girl in some faraway place at such moments. He told me he was not an exception. "I think of you."

It was such a beautiful letter, it seemed sacrilegious to throw his words away, so I've kept the letter for over thirty-five years. I've kept many such letters. One was from an entire company of cadets at a military academy.

Several evenings ago, a group of fellow cadets and myself decided to patronize a local theater, not particularly concerned about the subsequent title or subject. As fate inevitably dictates, it turned out to be a musical, and as we are necessarily orientated in a military frame-of-mind, this sort of film appealed to us about as much as the local wax museum. Nevertheless, we decided to remain and attempt to sleep throughout the balance of the feature.

I guess I could describe the ensuing reaction when you began "Sixteen Going On Seventeen", but both time and my limited vocabulary make this impossible. Needless to say, we are not sorry we went, and plan to go again. Often...

I received a great many letters back in the sixties from boys in their teens, and it has been wonderful for me over the past year to receive letters from those same 'bachelor dandies', now all grown up, but whom Liesl still touches, after all these years.

In 1964, I wrote you a fan letter after The Sound of Music *was first released. You sent me a letter and an autographed picture... I was a 10 year old boy then, and very thrilled. To this day I can't thank you enough.*

It's an amazing thing to me that an autograph or a photograph can make a lifelong impression on a young boy. Liesl has had many young fans.

I was seven years old when I saw the movie for the first time in 1965. I didn't want to go because I thought it was a sissy "girl movie". I wanted to stay home and play football in the backyard with my friends. So I pouted all the way to the theater.

Of course, I ended up loving the movie (though I made sure not to let my parents know that I liked it!). It's remained my favorite film. Plus, I developed a MAJOR crush on you that night in the theater, which has lasted to this day...

I don't know if these young men know what it means for me to hear such words today. It was wonderful receiving letters like this when I was younger, but now that I'm a grandmother, it's glorious!

I'm sure I'm like a million other guys who tell you that they have been in love with you forever. In my case, it happened on April 2, 1966, when I first saw The Sound of Music *as a high school senior. I wrote you a letter and you sent me back your hand-written 'form' letter and picture. How I cherished that picture!*

I had grand ideas of going to Hollywood and meeting you. Of course, we would fall in love instantly and live happily ever after. Ultimately, reality set in: it is a very long way from Kalamazoo, Michigan to California, especially for an eighteen-year-old with no car.

I have cherished you and the film for thirty-five years now - and will continue to do so, always...

I was astounded that this man still could remember the exact date when he first saw the film. It is through letters like his that I have come to know how strongly the film affects people when they first see it.

I am a huge fan, and have been since I first saw the movie in Kodiak, Alaska where I went to high school in 1965. It had a terrific impact on me and is still my all time favorite movie. I had a huge crush on you, and if they wouldn't have hired you because of your beautiful blue eyes that would have been a terrible shame for all of us! I was seventeen shortly after that (like Rolf), and had a girlfriend who I would sing "You are Sixteen Going on Seventeen" to. On an all-day hike on an island, she tripped and twisted her ankle and I was in heaven to be able to play the romantic "hero" as I carried her most of the way back to camp...

When we filmed the dance in the gazebo with Liesl and Rolf, I had a similar accident. The wardrobe department forgot to attach the rubber skids to my dance shoes, so when I jumped up onto the first bench, I slid right off, crashing through the glass windows of the gazebo. While I wasn't cut, I did sprain my ankle badly. I wish I could have had someone there to pick me up and carry me off like this young man did his girl! All I got was a vitamin B12 shot and an ace bandage...

A lot of men have written me that they would have made a different choice from the one Rolf does in the film. One of them had a familiar name.

My name is actually "Rolf", and since that name is somewhat uncommon here in the United States, I often get references to The Sound of Music *when people first meet me. I always tell them - if I had been "Rolf" in the movie, I would have gone to Switzerland with Liesl...*

I thought Rolf should have gone with us, too, and if you talk Dan Truhitte, who played the character in the movie, he would have been all for it. This mans's letter made me think that maybe we should start another club, one for "Rolf's."

Many people ask me if I was romantically involved with Dan during the filming. It's funny to think about it now, but I viewed Dan as being too young. He was twenty, a whole year younger than me. Back then, the notion of dating a younger man was, to me, unthinkable. I've received letters from fans who apparently had similar issues.

In 1965 when I first saw The Sound of Music, *I had just turned 22, just graduated from college, and was beginning life on my own. I fell in love with the movie and the music. And I developed a big crush on you through Liesl. I felt very guilty having such feelings toward a girl who was so much younger than me.*

In reading your book, I discovered that you are actually slightly older than me. ***SMILE***

That's right, I was legal! Legal Liesl. Though Dan and I never connected while we were making the film, he fell in love with and married my German stand-in. So in a way, he did marry "Liesl."

I hear from many people who fell in love while portraying the characters of Liesl and Rolf on stage.

Recently, an old boyfriend of mine got in contact with me and we met for the first time in nine years. We had grown up together and were childhood sweethearts until my family moved. He has never really left my thoughts.

At an audition for a school play, we sang and danced to "Sixteen Going On Seventeen" (we both got good roles in the play!). After our recent meeting, he left me a gift - a copy of your book, Forever Liesl. *With it was a note saying,*

"*It was lovely to see you - remember the audition?*
You have and always will be my Liesl,
Yours always, Rolf xx"

For many, the film and the love story between Liesl and Rolf is strongly linked to their memories of their own young love.

I was fifteen when The Sound of Music *made its road show debut. As you know, back then the blockbuster films of the Sixties were a very special event. The film would only play in one theater at a time in each town, and so we had to get reserved seats by mail, weeks ahead of time.* The Sound of Music *played exclusively at the Palms Theater in Phoenix for over a year and was sold out at every performance.*

It was my first date. I didn't drive, so my dad chauffeured us to the theater. On arrival, my date and I were met by immaculately uniformed ushers who escorted us to our seats. Everyone attending the film was dressed in suits and nice dresses as if they were attending an opera. The overture played in the theater up until the heavy, velvet curtains with gold tassels drew apart and the film began.

My girl and I were mesmerized. We fell in love that night. The memories of it are clear and vivid, enduring in a warm corner of my mind to this day.

"Liesl" was the object of many adolescent crushes.

When I saw the film in a theater, I was seated near a young mother and her daughter who was about ten. When Liesl came on screen, she whispered, "She's so pretty." I remember thinking, "I couldn't agree with you more." It was a critical juncture in my life. I was an adolescent beginning to notice girls and Liesl was my fantasy. I enjoyed a breathless dream that perhaps someday, she and I might actually be an 'item'...

I like that Liesl was the ideal that many young men aspired to love. As a character, she was young and bright, full of desire yet also full of innocence. She was pure and wholesome. For some young men, "she" provided a positive influence during their confusing adolescence.

I first saw the film in the mid-70's during the first re-release. All I remember is being pulled into the theater on a boring day in Kingsville, Texas, watching the movie, and walking out into the sunshine, mesmerized.

I was enchanted. It was a moment between getting beat up by bullies, killing others in tennis, doing homework, and listening to the Partridge Family for godssakes. Your character in the film hit me over the head like a ton of bricks. I was a 'wild and crazy' teen and this Liesl on the screen simply captivated me. That day, I walked out in despair, knowing I would never meet you.

Now, years later, I have the privilege of a semblance of that. I just wanted you to know you had a profound, positive influence on my life when I was a wild and crazy teen...

One thing that has amazed me this past year is hearing from young men for whom Liesl was their ideal long after the film was first released. Even though they know that I'm far past sixteen, they don't seem to mind.

As a preteen growing up during the eighties, I had an inconsolable crush on you. Although the film was made sometime before I was born, I grew up watching it on a near-daily basis, memorizing every song and bit of dialogue.

Naturally, many of my childhood peers didn't know who you were, so during one of my birthday parties, I screened the film in my parents' room and 'introduced' you as "that sixties starlet that I'm in love with."

I'm delighted to know you're alive and well, and, not to my surprise, you still have the same dimples and brilliant blue eyes that made my heart melt as a child so many years ago...

I guess as long as the movie is around, the illusion of me being sixteen will always exist, no matter how old I am.

I just watched your movie in the bus on the way to the Canadian Rocky Mountain Music Festival in Canada. I loved it so much, I requested we watch the movie on the way back, too! We sang a song titled, "Things That Never Die" with lyrics by Charles Dickens, and what it says is so true after watching you. You'll always be sixteen going on seventeen...

Well, with the help of a few plastic surgeons perhaps, but it's nice to know that at least on film, I'll always be that age.

Sometimes being "Liesl" has allowed me an opportunity to hear from people who I crossed paths with ever so briefly in life.

In the Spring of 1967, I was in Tahiti, staying at a resort when one day, the owner asked me to do him a favor. He wanted me to go snorkeling with a young lady whose husband had come down with something. I obliged, only to find out, I was going diving with "Liesl".

I will never forget the trusting way you took my hand to go into the water...

This man was able to find me because of my memoir. The book opened the door for many people to "find me" again. It has even managed to disrupt the schedule of at least one train.

I was eight years old when I saw the film. My parents had to DRAG me inside. Of course, I came out loving it, and thinking at the time I was in love with you.

I am a conductor for Amtrak and found your book left in a seat... picked it up and began to read. I think a few passengers missed their stops.

Reading your book took me back to a wonderful time..

I find bachelor dandies everywhere, all over the world.

I am thirty-one, from Mexico. I always had a crush on Liesl. What a wonderful movie "Sound of Music" is!!! When I have kids, they'll grow up with the movie, no question about it and they will love you just like me...

I hope so...

As Liesl in The Sound of Music *you were wonderful. As Charmian Carr, you are a special gift from God!*

I don't think I'll ever look upon myself as a gift from God, but I certainly believe the film has been, for many people, such a gift.

This probably sounds terribly corny, but one of the reasons for seeing this movie so many times was you! When I first saw The Sound of Music *in the sixties, I instantly fell in love with you on screen. I wrote you how much I loved you; I'm sure you know what it's like when you have an enormous crush on someone! I adored you then, and probably would now, as Liesl... or as Charmian!*

Actually, I didn't really know what it was like to have an enormous crush on someone back then. I'd had my first love, and was dating a wonderful young man who is still one of my closest friends to this day, but I had never experienced the kind of inconsolable love people frequently have written to me about until I was much older. Then, like the relationship between Liesl and Rolf, it didn't work out, but I learned through that experience, if one love doesn't prevail, another one will. I learned to never give up on the ideal of love.

While filming our documentary here today, I was asked during an interview what Nicky means to me. I hadn't expected to dissolve into tears on camera, but that's what happened.

Being back here in Salzburg, we are all experiencing some vulnerability. Our past is colliding with our present. So when I was asked about Nicky, I thought about what he has meant in my life and I was overcome with emotion.

Earlier in the day, he'd said that he was with me in the beginning and he would be with me until the end. With those words in my head, it was hard for me to articulate what he means to me without tears.

Nicky is truly my friend, and will be for as long as I'm on this planet, and probably will be even after I'm gone. I have a feeling whenever I die, he'll still be there beside me, ever after. He is a part of my soul, and I know his love for me is unconditional.

Why don't I marry Nicky? What we have with each other is not a husband and wife kind of love, but it's equally deep. Ours is the love lifelong friends have for each other. I don't think such relationships happen often in life, at least they haven't for me.

I feel so blessed to have Nicholas Hammond in my life. And I know I have *The Sound of Music* to thank for it.

Gazebo Dancers

It's raining in Salzburg, and since today happens to be the day we're filming inside the gazebo, it's as if the downpour has arrived on cue. This isn't the 'real' gazebo, of course. That was built on a soundstage in Los Angeles. But for millions, this glass-walled structure in Salzburg is *the* gazebo, and sitting here with raindrops sliding down the windows, I can easily evoke many memories of that day long ago when Dan and I danced in a "rainstorm". I feel sixteen again, or at the very least, twenty-one.

Filming the dance with Liesl and Rolf in the gazebo started out as a near disaster, and ended as one of the most thrilling moments in my life. It was the last complete scene to be shot for *The Sound of Music*. I'd rehearsed for seven months to do that dance. I loved it and couldn't wait for the filming to begin. The last thing I expected was that I'd go flying through the glass windows on the first take, but that's exactly what happened. I remember sitting on the floor, with glass all around me, thinking, "This can't be happening."

It was a technically difficult dance, very athletic, and over the years, when I've seen it on film, I've grown more and more impressed with the artistry of choreographers Marc Breaux and Dee Dee Wood. I recently reconnected with Marc at an event in Palm Springs, and I found myself tearing up as I introduced him.

This man helped create the dance that will always define me. Every time I watch the scene, as the incredible Rodgers and Hammerstein music builds to a crescendo and 'Rolf' lifts me off the bench, spinning me in his arms, I get goosebumps. To be able to publically acknowledge Marc, a World War II pilot turned choreographer, was very meaningful for me. I owe him so much.

Marc and Dee Dee's genius has inspired many people. Over the years, I have learned that I am not the only gazebo dancer out there. From the day *The Sound of Music* was released, people have mimicked that dance, losing themselves in joyful leaps from bench to bench. I call these people 'gazebo dancers.' When they write to me, I lovingly warn them that gazebo dancing can be a very risky business.

A tour guide here in Salzburg told me the story of an eighty-two year old gazebo dancer. She hopped up onto the benches of the famous gazebo, and as she tried to leap from one bench to the next, she slipped and broke her hip. "She was not the first person to attempt this," the guide said, shaking his head. "Every day there was another one." He told me they were easy to spot, these women and girls who would enter the gazebo with a gleam in their eye, leaping up onto a bench without a moment's hesitation.

In an effort to avoid injuries to other gazebo dancers, the gazebo is now locked. "Only we tour guides have the key."

"That's probably wise," I said.

He shrugged. "Yes, but if they can't jump in this one, they just find someplace else to do your dance."

He's right. I hear from these gazebo dancers all the time.

Mum said that in Prep (kindergarten) I jumped up at assembly and started singing "I am sixteen, going on seventeen" in front of 1000 kids, and then I tried to do that step from bench to bench which resulted in 14 stitches and a sprained ankle!

Gazebo dancing seems to be a problem the world over. I recently heard from a mother in Australia who was concerned about her children.

The other day, I walked into our lounge to find that our young daughter had arranged our furniture in a circular formation, and was leaping from seat to seat singing, "I am sixteen going on seventeen." My main concern was that she was being watched by our two year old who would not have had the same ability to make the leaps! Any suggestions?

Being the grandmother of a two-year-old, I would have the same concern. I can envision my little Emma going for it, trying to do those leaps. The other day she sang me "Do-Re-Mi" and "Edelweiss." I know "Sixteen Going on Seventeen" is coming next.

I've heard enough of these stories now that I'm beginning to think that the video and DVD boxes should have some sort of warning label that says: do not try this in your own homes.

It isn't just all those "Liesl's" out there who are at risk. "Rolf's" are in peril, too.

I grew up watching The Sound of Music. *I usually would play Brigitta because my mom would braid my hair just like her, and my sister would always get the part of Liesl. But when Liesl and Rolf dance in the gazebo, guess who got the part of Rolf? Me. When Liesl did a kick, so did my sister, and she usually kicked me in the face...*

Fortunately, not all gazebo dancers suffer injuries. One woman told me that when she was little and her parents would take her to the zoo, she would pretend to be Liesl, jumping from bench to bench, just like I did with Rolf, and that her father would hold her hand to help her along the way. It's such a lovely image for me to conjure up that it makes me reluctant to discourage gazebo dancers. The dance is capable of filling one's soul with great joy.

I used to act out all of Liesl's scenes and the one in the gazebo was my favorite. I made my parents move all the furniture into a circle around our living room at least twice a month and I danced exactly in step with you. I don't think I've ever had so much fun as a child than during my "performances" as Liesl in my living room...

These letters take me back to a time when I was young, when, if I felt sad, I would dance. I would put on music, especially Debussy's

"Afternoon of a Fawn", and I would dance, and it would always transport me to a different place, away from my worries. I was so happy and content in those moments, and so involved with the music, as if it was coming from deep inside me. I think that is what these people are telling me the film has done for them.

Dear "Liesl",

Like many children, I grew up re-enacting the gazebo scene. I played "couch-coffee table", jumping back and forth between the couch and coffee table rather than gazebo benches, but I was so happy.

I understand completely, and it makes me so happy that acting out that dance can bring contentment into these girls lives.

When I was growing up, my next-door neighbor and I used to pretend we were Liesl and Rolf, and would jump around from picnic bench to picnic bench in our garage. It's a wonder we didn't hurt ourselves! But it was so much fun...

It's sweet to envision children acting out that dance, to know that it's a fantasy they want to leap into, like a *Mary Poppins* sidewalk chalk drawing. It's a marvelous legacy to Marc and Dee Dee (who also, by coincidence, choreographed *Mary Poppins*) that children (and adults!) are re-enacting their gazebo dance, even now.

Some gazebo dancers don't just mimic the dance I did with Rolf. They incorporate the whole film into their lives, like this young woman and her family.

I am 27 now and have loved The Sound of Music *for as long as I can remember. I forced/dragged my two younger sisters and three cousins to watch it over and over, and eventually to act it out. As twelve through three year olds, we marched down the stairs, leapt from couch to chair to coffee table in our attempts to be you, and sang every song and knew every line for every character. We knew and still know every expression, every gesture. Even our parents, who initiated this love of the film within us, thought we were absolutely nuts.*

At the dinner table, when all of us were together, when asked questions we kids would always answer with lines from the movie. "Jennifer, how was your day at school?" would be answered with, "I don't know, I DON'T KNOW!" like Maria talking to the Mother Abbess, with the exact inflection and desperation Julie uses. It became a great joke to all the children and a somewhat happy aggravation to the parents.

I love hearing how people make games out of the film.

We used to sit as close to the television as we could when the movie started and try to win the "Who can see Maria on the mountain first?" game. And then we would take turns and pick out a von Trapp child and watch them for the entire film to see if we noticed anything unusual that they did in the background or off to the side. "Check out what Friedrich does here!"

We warped my parents' "Sound of Music" album listening to it over and over as we "Liesled" our way around the backyard picnic benches. Our deck was the puppet show theater, with our Ernie and Cookie monster puppets doubling as the lonely goatherd Marrionettes.

I don't know what it is about that movie, but I wanted to tell you, it still brings me unlimited joy!

Another woman wrote me about similar games she played with her sisters.

My sisters and I grew up with The Sound of Music. *We all wanted to be Liesl, and would constantly sing "Sixteen Going on Seventeen". And we invented this game.*

We would each have to say a line from The Sound of Music *in a certain amount of time. The game took a long time, because we all knew the lines backwards and forwards! Now, we are all in our twenties, married, and we still love* The Sound of Music, *and, every once in a while, we'll still play our game.*

That could be a three hour game. I wouldn't suggest anyone try to play it against Angela. I think she knows the lines better than Ernest Lehman - and he wrote the screenplay!

There seems to be a special bond between sisters and this film. Together, they become gazebo dancers.

I am 25 years old now, but I remember watching the movie over and over with my younger sister. We would pause the movie, frame by frame, as we tried to learn the dance which Liesl and Rolf did in the gazebo. I believe the film drew my sister and I both to our love of music and to performing on stage...

Of course, there are times when the desire to be a gazebo dancer isn't a shared one between siblings.

When I was nine, we put on a "production" of The Sound of Music *in my best friend's basement. I insisted on being Liesl, of course. My sister was coerced into playing Gretl, but she refused to cry during the storm scene (she was five). Unfortunately, when we shoved her out on the 'stage', she wacked her lip on the corner of the makeshift bed (several cardboard boxes covered by a sheet) so she ended up crying after all...*

All these people are being injured playing "Sound of Music." We can't get that warning label on fast enough!

Many children fantasize about being part of the von Trapp family. An One family of girls dreamt of becoming the five sisters we portrayed.

My four sisters and I used to pretend that we were the von Trapp girls. We even talked about forming a singing group together because we wanted to be like the von Trapp family. I was Louisa because I was second in age, but I always wished I was Liesl because you had your own song.

The Trapp Family Singers have inspired many families to want to follow in their footsteps.

My mom and my sisters and I used to sing together all the time. We thought we could give the Lennon Sisters a run for their money. As a twelve year old, The Sound of Music *brought all my romantic notions to life. Here was a story about a whole family who sang and the world embraced them. I loved it!*

And the female heroines were based on real women who were strong. What could be more powerful to a young girl than a woman role model who helped save children. Such role models were rare back in the Sixties.

I loved that this was a story about a family who stuck together, overcoming all odds. I had a close family and always wanted to believe in the strength of our connection to each other. I just wanted you to know how much I could lose myself in this story as a child. I could actually feel like I was there, I was a part of it. I'd love to be able to recapture that youthful ability and to once again live vicariously in the Austrian hills with the von Trapps.

Sometimes, just singing a simple song is all a gazebo dancer needs to fulfill a childhood fantasy.

As a child, I used to play "Sixteen Going on Seventeen" over and over on the stereo and sing your part at the top of my lungs. I would imagine myself singing that song to an audience and reliving Liesl's magic. Well, my dream came true. My husband's weekend business is music entertainment and karaoke. When I found out he had your song on a new collection of movie classics I was in heaven.

Together one night we sang "Sixteen" to an audience and I had chills as I played out my childhood fantasy, singing the same words that Liesl did so many years ago.

Other gazebo dancers dance only in their dreams.

During the dreaded middle school years, I was at least three inches taller than anyone in my class, boy or girl, and was as uncoordinated as anything. When I got mononucleosis in the sixth grade, I watched The Sound of Music *a countless number of times and always fell asleep dreaming that I could dance as gracefully as Liesl, with a man who was taller than I...*

Even a simple dress can allow people to 'live the dream.'

I first saw The Sound of Music *in 1970 when I was in our community theater production of the musical on stage. The entire cast went to see the movie when on the big screen. That summer I saw the movie six times and was moved to tears each time. Of course, my favorite part of the movie has always been the gazebo scene with Liesl and Rolf. Every time I ever needed a special dress for an occasion, I always looked for one with a flowing skirt like Liesl's in that scene...*

Few things touch me more than hearing from people about how they loved the film as a child, and how their own children now respond to it with equal passion. In this day of high-stimulation high-tech, it's gratifying to know that an old-fashioned story about family and love can still touch children deep in their hearts.

I grew up loving The Sound of Music *and singing all the songs. Now my two-year-old daughter is just as enchanted with the film. She likes for us to act out "So Long, Farewell" on our stairs. She pretends to be Gretl and puts her head down on her arms at the top of the stairs. Then my role is to play Liesl and pick her up and carry her to her bedroom, meanwhile singing all the parts to the song. This was all her idea, but I think I did the same thing when I was a little girl...*

I love that the film speaks right to the heart of people's dreams and inspires them to play.

On this journey to Salzburg, I learned that the gazebo is not only the site for dancers, but also for marriage proposals. The gazebo was, after all, not only the place where Liesl experiences her first kiss, but also where the Captain and Maria admit their love for one another (which I think is one of the most romantic scenes of all time.) So the gazebo represents both young love and mature love, and it came as no surprise to me that "Sound of Music Tour" guides frequently see a man down on one knee asking a girl to marry him. "It's incredible," says my guide. "We see them all the time."

It's amazing to me that a set, developed for a scene in a play and then incorporated into a movie, could become a symbol of something special for so many people. Yet, the gazebo is certainly something special for me, symbolizing many things: the excitement of making the film, the joy of dancing, the sense of accomplishment after a lot of hard work, and the sadness of endings (since it was the last scene we shot). But mostly, when I see a gazebo, it reminds me of one of the biggest thrills of my life.

I remember every minute of the day we filmed the dance as if it was yesterday. I didn't want to do the famous "Weeeee!" that Liesl squeals as she comes out of the gazebo into the rain. I protested to Bob Wise that I thought it would look silly, but he was adamant that it remain. So I began the day excited about the dance and hopeful I wouldn't look too ridiculous squealing in the rain.

A friend's son once told me that he felt someone should invent a Liesl doll with one of those strings that you pull causing the doll to say something. "When you pull on Liesl's string," he said, "She'd squeal 'Weeeee!.'" There are Liesl dolls out there, but none like the one this boy envisioned. I'm grateful that no toy company ever thought of it.

But, the "Weeeee" no longer bothers me. It gives me chills. For on that day in 1964, when I slipped off the bench and crashed through the gazebo's glass window, it was a moment that would change my life.

I knew as I sat on the floor of the soundstage with stage hands and glass all around that I was going to get up and do that dance even if my leg was broken. It was my *job*. While we waited for the studio doctor to arrive, Bob and Saul discussed the possibility of getting a double and filming the scene from a distance, but I was adamant I would finish what I had been hired to do. I was Liesl and this was my dance.

The doctor taped me up and said I could give it a try. I grit my teeth and put some weight on my leg and didn't fall over. I smiled. "It's fine."

All through the day I danced. Though my ankle hurt, it never failed me in those leaps. With each successive take, a feeling grew inside of me. I was no longer the dependant and uncertain girl I'd been when I was hired to play Liesl. I had changed. The accident in the gazebo was a gift. It taught me something I hadn't known about myself.

On the final take, as I came out of the gazebo into the rain with my arms stretched wide, squealing, "Weeeeee!", all the union men on the film crew, the gaffers and the riggers and the grips and the gophers, stood up and gave me a standing ovation. They'd never done that before, on any other scene, with any other actor, and I was thrilled to the depths of my soul by their gesture.

It's a rare moment in life when you know, you <u>know</u>, you've been transformed. It happened for me that day in the gazebo. I'd gone from being a girl to a woman, from a rookie to a professional. I'll never forget how glorious that realization was and the validation of that crew.

For me, to dance in that gazebo was the stuff dreams are made of.

I hope everyone has a chance to be a gazebo dancer, at least once in their life. To be a gazebo dancer is very simple. Whether you're five or ninety-five, you can be one. All you have to do is remember how to pretend, and then imagine yourself being inside your best dream.

Just promise me you'll be careful as you leap from bench to bench.

Thunderstorms

As much fun as it is to be back in Salzburg, being here has made all seven of us vulnerable. As Nicky has so aptly put it, when we filmed the movie here in 1964, it was in the spring and everything was new. We have returned to film this documentary in the autumn, and there is a reflection of ourselves in the natural beauty which surrounds us. Time has passed. We are middle-aged. It's impossible to be here together and not reflect on what has happened during the years in between, and on what we wish might have been different in our lives. Some of the dreams we had as young people are unfulfilled and some of the people we loved are gone. It is not always easy to go home.

There have been personal moments for each of us when we've felt a need to pull apart and privately reconcile our pasts with the present, to recognize: some things have been forever lost. Salzburg, this unchanged city of our youth, is a mirror for us.

I suppose it is no different for anyone on a journey back in time. Returning is intoxicating and joyful, yet also bittersweet. In some ways, my life has not turned out as I thought it would back in 1964. I believed I'd be married forever, that I'd always be happy, that I'd never be alone. I believed that no one I loved was ever going to die. But life isn't like that. Everyone faces difficult times. Everyone has thunderstorms.

I sometimes wondered if I was going to survive the grief I felt during the times of loss. A handful of things kept me afloat: music and Labradors and good friends and family. Being here in Salzburg has given me a chance to reflect on them all.

I always knew that the film had millions of fans around the world, but it wasn't until I began to work on <u>Forever Liesl</u> that I began to realize that *The Sound of Music* was much more than just a favorite movie. Following the book's release, the letters began to arrive. I learned that the film has actually helped people cope with their thunderstorms.

Sometimes, this happens in a literal way. One family wrote me about how, when they were huddled in their basement during a tornado alert, with the wind howling above them, their youngest child asked fearfully, "What's that song we're supposed to sing when we're afraid?" And the whole family began to sing "My Favorite Things" and the storm was soon past.

But other times, the thunderstorm is a profoundly painful moment which doesn't go away quickly. Losing a loved one, coping with a grave illness; these things don't go away with the wind. I have been amazed by the stories people have shared with me about the way in which the film has helped them through such times. These stories are, to me, the greatest gift I will ever receive for having been a part of *The Sound of Music.*

When I was in Chicago on my book tour, a man handed me his book to sign and said quietly, "You have no idea what the film has meant to my family." As I sat with my pen poised over his book, he proceeded to tell me a story.

The Sound of Music was his mother's favorite film. Diagnosed with a terminal illness, she was hospitalized, and was understandably very frightened of dying. The man wanted to do something to make his mother more comfortable, and finally, he thought to bring the video of *The Sound of Music* to the hospital.

There in his mother's hospital room, the family sat and watched the film together with her, and for three hours, his mother forgot about her pain. She laughed and cried tears of joy and hummed along with the songs, and when it was over, she drifted into a peaceful sleep. He said the film worked better than all the morphine and Valium they were giving her.

She died quietly the next morning.

I was crying by then, trying to sign the man's book without getting it wet with my tears. I tried to express to him how it made me feel to hear that the film made his mother's last hours peaceful, to let him know how humbling it is to have been a part of something that could bring someone out of their pain and their fear.

It lifts me tremendously to hear how the film has eased people's suffering. One woman told me how the film kept her company during a long hospital stay, and no matter how much pain she was in, "Sixteen Going On Seventeen" could always make her smile. The film and the music can be as powerful an antidote to pain as any medication.

I am twenty-one years old. Last year, I had viral double pneumonia and was in a coma for five weeks. My total hospital stay was three months. I watched the movie to help keep my spirits up and keep me going. I also would listen to the soundtrack and that would relax me after very intense physical therapy to ensure that I would be able to walk again...

The inspiration people receive from the film is something they feel compelled to share.

My mother saw the film for the first time the night before she had major back surgery, and it so encouraged her that she took the whole family to see it with her when she was able to return home.

It has helped people surmount the most difficult of circumstances.

The Sound of Music is the movie I turned to for comfort when my son was diagnosed with a rare disease and I felt numb. It always made me feel better - I could count on it. And my son and I listened to the music when he went for his treatments. It gave me inspiration. The film will be something I turn to in my last moments...

To know that the film has helped people rise above emotional pain and, for a short time at least, escape to something hopeful and familiar makes me feel incredible. I am frequently awestruck by the way in which *The Sound of Music* has played a role in people's lives.

I read your book while coping with my brother's terminal illness. Your memoirs happily carried me away to another time and place, and helped me start smiling again.

I remember many years ago reading a book written by a woman describing her mother's terminal illness. Shortly before she died, the mother whispered to her daughter that she wanted her to sing the songs from The Sound of Music. *Though she was a woman of faith, she didn't request prayer or scripture or hymns. She requested "The Sound of Music."*

There, in her hospital room, this woman sang for her mother. Perhaps in her mother's mind, heaven looked like the Austrian Alps. Memories of that film eased her suffering at an important time, and I've never forgotten that. How wonderful for you to have been a part of a film that not only entertained, but also brought comfort to people at times of distress.[1]

Sometimes, the film simply offers a reminder of values that people cherish. It can give them something to believe in. A young man felt the movie helped him through a difficult period.

About a year ago, unknown to me, a family member I was living with was doing drugs. Things were getting pretty ugly, and for some much needed encouragement, I went to the local library and got the 30th anniversary edition of the film. Watching it ended up giving me a sense of hope that I had lost. The Sound of Music has done that for me on a number of occasions. It has truly had a profound impact on my life...

---

1 The book is <u>Mourning Song</u> by Joyce Landorf Heatherley, pub.1974 by Baker Books.

A counselor wrote me about how she was helped by the film as a child, and then how she found the film valuable in helping people she treats in her practice.

I was 13 when The Sound of Music *came out. I had an abusive, alcoholic mom and a workaholic dad. I watched the film over and over, and it made me feel better. I am now a therapist and many of my clients tell me this movie changed their hurting lives...*

In my memoir, I briefly chronicle some of my own mother's struggles in life. Having personally dealt with an alcoholic parent, my heart goes out to people who have coped with similar situations.

I have a special place in my heart for The Sound of Music. *It was my father's favorite film. Like your mom, my father related more to alcohol than anything else, but I treasure the connection that I feel with him when I watch the movie and hear his (and my) favorite song, "Edelweiss."*

My father died in 1987, and when a friend asked me if I missed him, I answered, "Not really, because his pain and my worries were buried with him." Ironically, The Sound of Music *played that next day and I cried my eyes out during Christopher Plummer's solo of "Edelweiss." I realized that I did miss him; the things that I liked and the things that were never meant to be.*

Fatefully, a friend bought me a music box for Christmas just two weeks later. Without knowing the connection, she chose "Edelweiss"...

The film can make people feel a connection to a lost parent.

Watching The Sound of Music *is a great comfort after my mother's death from cancer last year. It was "our" special movie.*

Or it can simply help them through a bad day or a bout with the flu, like this woman in Australia.

A year ago, a new roommate moved in to my house that I didn't know very well. One evening I heard Julie Andrews' voice floating from her room. "What's going on?" I yelled through the door.

"I'm watching The Sound of Music!*" she yelled back.*

Soon, we were both watching the film together and telling each other about how the film touched our lives. It turned out she watches it whenever she feels down, and now, whenever one of us is upset or ill, we put on her tape of The Sound of Music...

Many have written about how they gained solace from the film in their youth.

The Sound of Music *helped me through a difficult childhood. My younger brother had diabetes and my dad was away during most of our growing up years and we were quite poor. I grew up fast and never really 'stayed' a child for long, as Mom was ill a lot.*

I was closest to your age (15 going on 16) when the film came out, and I wanted to be like you. I saved my babysitting money and took the bus to San Francisco to see the film twelve times. As the lights of the theater went down and the first glimpses of the snow-covered Alps appeared, I was once again transported to a realm of great beauty where I felt wrapped in the warm embrace of kindness and love.

The love of family and the values the film represents still stand up today in a world not so kind or innocent. I just wanted you to know how much the film meant to me, and how for a period of my life it kept me sane and gave me a focus to cling to...

The film has helped many young people not only cope with difficult circumstances, but to find a new way of life to aspire to.

The first time I saw the movie, I was at that age when girls search for something or someone to model themselves after. I had always been "daddy's girl", but when my parents got divorced, I saw the real person my father was.

Even with that disappointment, living with my mother was no comfort. From my earliest memories in my playpen, I can see my mother kneeling down outside of the bars, hissing between her teeth, "I hope you never get married. You'd be better off alone all your life." I know now that she was mentally ill, but had no idea about such things at the time.

When I first saw The Sound of Music, *I didn't know I was looking for a role model. I didn't even know what that term meant. But in the character of Liesl, I saw such beauty and poise, such innocense and joy. None of these things did I have.*

But that grace that you brought to the role - I could try to incorporate that into my personality, I was sure. I had been such an angry child, and was prone to hit and be mean. But I did try to incorporate a gentleness into my personality and posture. I still had brown eyes and red hair, but I began being a teenager with a different will to be gracious, and with God's help, accomplished it to a degree.

I never saw you in anything else until I was married and saw a TV commercial you had done. I don't remember even what it was for, but it was like seeing an old friend I'd lost track of. I'd often wondered what happened to the actress who embodied femininity to me.

Many more years would pass before I stumbled across your book in a store. I can't express to you how much it meant to me to read it. I wished I could have known you all those years, and now, I feel like I almost did.

This summer, my mother passed away. With the help of the hospice, I really came to see my mother's life with more clarity, coming to terms with the fact that my mother was not the best person in the world. But I now know that without her, and yes, even the way she treated me, I would not be the person I am today (who I really like very much). It was a very healing thing. I sensed from your own story a similar feeling, and I was glad to learn that the girl I had so wanted to be like had preceded me in this as well. I completed a very sentimental journey reading your book.

I will never be in the position of impacting millions of people as you have done, but I will be able to impact a few. And that is good enough for me. Thank you...

I am humbled by such gratitude...

Many parents have written to tell me about the special bond their children have with the film.

My thirteen-year-old daughter has cerebral palsy, is in an electric wheelchair and is non-verbal so speaks on a computerized augmentative communication device called a Liberator. She is extremely beautiful, bright, social, and a very hard worker! She certainly has her fair share of life's challenges, but meets them with a vengeance, and is a true inspiration to all who meet her. Well guess what! She's an avid "Sound of Music" fan. She and I never get our fill of watching the movie.

I hardly ever watch movies more than once, and when I do, subsequent viewings seem to last longer, with less enjoyment. "Music" flies by, and we just become more and more endeared to it. I get such a kick out of Amy putting in the video all by herself, then beckoning me to "come here and watch the movie with me", with her little side finger motion. Amy's and my hearts just soar every time we watch the Captain dance the Laendler with Maria.

I just want to say thanks for this incredible movie which has given my daughter and me so many countless hours of joy...

That *The Sound of Music* can help enrich a child's life means a great deal to me. That it can actually help a child in some way is priceless.

I was a huge fan of the film as a kid (and remain so), drawing countless pictures of the von Trapp children; now my two daughters are big fans, drawing their own countless pictures of the von Trapps.

This story is about my older, six-and-a-half year old daughter. She is adorable and, as she currently has a diagnosis of high-functioning autism (though she is well on the way to recovery), she is a bit "different".

When she was 4 years old I decided to introduce her to my favorite childhood movie just to see if she would like the musical numbers (I knew the story would be hard to grasp) and she did. Big time. And can you guess her favorite number? "Sixteen Going on Seventeen." As kids with autism tend to develop an over-focus on certain things, your dance routine with Rolf dominated our lives for at least six months to a year.

Her very favorite activity to do with me during these months was to have the two of us gallop back and forth a couple times holding hands and singing a few lines from the song. Then she (pretending to be Rolf) would kiss me (pretending to be Liesl) then run off, turn around and laugh uproariously as I went "Wheeeeeeeee!" What got even funnier was that, around this time, she was diagnosed with a systemic yeast overgrowth (common in autism) and from all the grown-up conversation, caught wind of the word "yeast." Well, she thought that was the funniest word she ever heard so, upon her request, I changed "Wheeeeeeeeee!" to "Yeeeaaast!" (I've often told my husband that living with autism is like living your life in a quirky, independent film...)

Until that time, she had never gotten the hang of greeting people. But, one day, she was looking out the window and saw me across the street coming home; without thinking I opened my arms wide--a la Liesl--and mouthed "Yeeeaaast!" to her. She did the same back to me and that was how we greeted each other for a long time. (Now she cheerfully says "hello" and "hi").

In addition to acting out the number, we have a hilarious photo of her watching the famous "Wheeeee!" on TV. Her arms are bolted straight over her head and her expression is pure joy. Somebody who didn't know better would assume that her favorite team had just scored a touchdown.

It has helped give strength to many children during stormy times.

I just want to thank you for brightening up my daughter's life for the past year. She is nine, and was diagnosed with Tourettes Syndrome a year ago. For months, it was an emotional roller-coaster. And then, she found comfort and happiness in listening to the soundtrack and watching the video of The Sound of Music. *She would act out or sing all the parts which would have a calming effect on her.*

When she was going through the initial diagnosis and dealing with so many doctors, she was giving up, and I would ask her, "What would Liesl or Maria do? Would they give up hope?"

The Sound of Music *taught her about herself, the strength she has inside, and she has in turn inspired other children to watch and appreciate the film. We plan on getting her a dog and she was trying to think of an original cute name. She has decided to name the dog "Liesl". I hope you take this as a compliment...*

I do!

Generally, I hear these inspirational stories via letters or emails. It is rare that I am able to personally witness the power of *The Sound of Music.* Recently, I was invited to attend a community production of the play in Sonoma, California. In the course of arranging the details, I learned that one of the children in the production had brain cancer. I sent a copy of my book, along with some prayers, to five-year-old Rachel.

Three months later, when I traveled to Sonoma to see the play, I learned she wasn't well enough to participate on stage. But Rachel and her older sister Chelsea came to meet me at my hotel. I was expecting to see this very ill child, but Rachel walked all on her own right up to me with her beautiful smile, stared at my face, and asked a little doubtfully, "Are you *really* Liesl?"

"Yes," I said, and I knelt down beside her and sang to her. "I am sixteen, going on seventeen..."

When I finished, she threw her arms around me and hugged me tight. "You are her!"

Later, we drove to the theater together. It was an hour before the play was to begin, and when we stepped inside the door, the two hundred other children involved in the production were waiting for us. They jumped to their feet and began to cheer and Rachel squeezed my hand as we walked in together.

The director asked if I'd be willing to go on stage for the final song of the play, a reprise of "Do-Re-Mi", and when I nodded, she knelt down and asked Rachel if she'd like to go, too. So at the end of the play, holding Rachel's hand, I walked out on stage for the first time in years. As we began to sing to the audience, Rachel tugged my skirt. "Would you pick me up?" I did, and in that instant, multi-colored confetti dropped from the ceiling, and Rachel hugged me tight as she sang at the top of her voice in my arms. "Doe, a deer, a female deer, ray a drop of golden sun..."

It was a perfect moment: the joy of all those children singing, and the wonderful child in my arms, loving every minute of it. I watched her reaching skyward, laughing, making the most of every second, and her love of life and her courage inspired me. It is no coincidence that her nickname is "Rae". She is a drop of golden sun.

I don't know if Rachel knew it, or her parents and sister knew it, or if the folks who organized the Broadway Bound Kids production of the play knew it, but it meant everything to me to be a part of their production and to witness firsthand how *The Sound of Music* continues to give such joy to people, especially children.

Rachel and her family are facing their own thunderstorm, and *Music* is one of the things that helps them enjoy each day. This family, and other's like them, have helped me through my own stormy days. They have reminded me how precious life is and that sometimes, the best antidote for the most frightening things we face in life is to fill our hearts with song.

Family

Dear Charmy,

I'll see you in Austria! I can't wait. I don't know if it's possible to recreate or relive wonderful experiences... but this is as close as one can get.

Your loving sister,

Louisa

I received this email from Heather the day before we left for Salzburg, and I loved her salutation. It *does* feel like we're a family, and it's been a wonderful thing to have known each other all these years.

It happened gradually. When we were making the film, I spent a great deal of my free time working on the documentary, *Salzburg: Sight and Sound*, and also being with the other adults. But on the set, I really felt like a big sister to the six other actors who played the von Trapp children. It would be time to shoot and I'd start to tell them to settle down. "Okay, stop fooling around. Don't touch that, you'll get electrocuted. Keep your hands to yourself. Come on now, they're ready to shoot."

Today, I wouldn't dare tell them what to do. When we were filming the movie, I was the tallest of the group (at least before Nicky grew half a foot), but now I'm the shortest. I'm no longer the *big* sister, so I don't give them directions anymore. They might get mad at me!

In 1965, after the film was released I was frequently traveling, but the kids would get together on special occasions, particularly birthdays, and if I was in town, I'd join them. Then Twentieth Century Fox started reuniting us, first at the one year anniversary, then at the fifth, and pretty soon we began to get together on our own.

Certainly, the film is part of our glue. It brought us together, and I think it keeps us together. Every family has something that unites them, whether it's aging parents or children or special occasions. We "film von

Trapps" are no different. *The Sound of Music* means so much to people, that over the years we've reached out to each other, if only to muse about what the mutual experience of 'being a von Trapp' has been like for us. We're the only ones who know what it was like to be a part of not only making it, but of the phenomenon that followed. The fact that we have remained close is as important to some fans of the film as it is to us.

I am so happy to know that your co-star siblings are like a second family to you. As a very little girl, I always believed that you and the other children WERE siblings. As 22, I can now still believe this...

So we are a family, the seven of us. For me, I really felt our bond for the first time at the 25th reunion in London. By then, I was in my mid-forties, and the gap had narrowed between us. We had the common experiences of marriage and children and the ups-and-downs of careers. This made me feel closer to all of them in a way I never had before. We didn't just have the film to talk about: we also had the problems and joys of everyday life that we shared. Like any family, some of us get along with each other better than with others. Age seems to play a role. Nicky and I are close, Heather and Angela are best friends, and Duane and Debbie and Kym are a tight knit group.

Being back in Salzburg together as adults is a surprisingly emotional experience. I have watched a closeness develop between Nicky and Duane, and between all the 'girls'. Every night in the hotel, it is like a giant slumber party. We are so lucky to have this time alone with each other. It's a miracle, really, that we're all still alive and healthy, thirty-six years after our big adventure, and it's wonderful to be able to laugh and talk and hug, and even regress, every day here. Angela and Heather used to play this patty-cake game between takes back in 1964, and they have cracked me up by doing the same thing now. And they're still good at it!

Every evening, our dinners run late into the night. One evening in particular, we got the impression that the restaurant staff thought we were a tad obnoxious. It wasn't our fault. A red balloon appeared on the table (actually, it wasn't really a red balloon, it was something that looked like a red balloon), and it was blown up and was being bounced around to shrieks of laughter, when a rather stuffy manager poked her head in to see if all was okay. Unfortunate timing. Of course, our British film crew was entirely responsible for such transgressions. The seven of us are far too sophisticated for such silly behavior.

Many of Salzburg's hotels have pictures of us as children from the film hanging in their lobbies, and Nicky quipped as we were making our exit that night that he wouldn't be surprised if the hotel put a mug shot of what we look like now over the picture of us in the lobby with a sign warning, "If these people show up, don't let them back in!"

I love that the seven of us grew into a family. To me, family is what life is all about, and this has guided me throughout my life, not only personally, but professionally. It is the sole reason I never made another feature film.

I always wished you had done more movies. You are my all time favorite beautiful woman, and I could easily picture you with Veronica Lake's hair and red lipstick, wearing a classic gown... Why didn't you make any other movies?

I didn't stop acting, I just started doing something else: being a mom. When I was on the *Sound of Music* set, I learned that acting requires a total commitment of your time, and I knew, once I was married and thinking of starting a family, that I couldn't raise children well and make movies at the same time. It was an easy decision. When I was pregnant with my first child, I stopped acting. When my daughters were old enough, I began to do commercials. I went from being Liesl to selling Ex-Lax.

I first saw The Sound of Music *as a 14-year-old in 1965 in Houston. I (and thousands of other boys) had a huge secret crush on you. I remember in the late seventies, I saw an Ex-Lax commercial on t.v., and I told my brother, "That lady looks like Liesl!" Was it you? If so, you did a very fine job.*

I'm flattered to know that I was convincing at selling a laxative! I ended up making over two hundred commercials, selling everything from cat food to milk to chocolate chip cookies to cough syrup. This worked great with being a mom. The jobs were short, just a day or two usually, and I was almost always home when my girls came home.

I've never regretted my choice of leaving the film industry, and I am so proud of my grown daughters. Nothing else I do in life will ever approach what being their mother means to me. Memories of our times together are the ones I cherish most in life.

The Sound of Music is part of so many families memories. For some, watching it together just once was a singularly memorable event. For others, watching the film is a frequent family habit or a holiday tradition. One woman wrote me about the annual ritual she has with her daughter of watching *The Sound of Music* every year on Christmas night. Last year, they went to watch it and couldn't find the tape. It turned out the woman's husband had taken the video to his mother at her nursing home. When she died a month later, the woman imagined her mother-in-law having watched the film during her last days, and was happy for the joy she felt it hopefully brought her.

The film connects many people to cherished loved ones they miss.

The Sound of Music *was my Grandpa's favorite movie, so when I would sleep over at my grandparent's house, I would get to stay up late and watch the movie. Now that he has died, I am so grateful for that time!*

I hear such stories again and again.

It was my mom's favorite movie. In fact, four days prior to her death from stomach cancer in 1995, she was so proud to be able to watch the entire movie from the hospital. It was definitely her dying wish.

Now the love and legacy lives on in me. It is a precious time capsule holding my mother in my heart. I now have two little girls who love the movie. I can only hope that someday, when I am gone, they will have me with them, along with their grandmother whom they never met, when they watch the movie...

The film can be the catalyst for a revered childhood memory.

It was December of 1965, and it had not been a good Christmas... We had driven hundreds of miles to my grandmother's home where our hopes for lots of snow and time with cousins had been dashed by lots of rain. We spent way too much time by ourselves in a small tar paper house for the holidays. In fact, my grandmother hadn't even bothered to get a tree and had no decorations, ornaments, anything Christmas.

My dad was always *busy, but he always stopped at Christmas to spend time with us, to hike and cut down a tree, target shoot, and have a family dinner. None of that happened in 1965. But on Christmas Eve, he determined to turn the whole miserable thing around. He actually drove to a closed Christmas tree stand late at night and pulled a tree out of the trash. He brought it home and made paper ornaments 'til the wee hours of the morning. And on Christmas morning he announced that we would do something special and go out to the movies... which was something we never did.*

We saw The Sound of Music.

I was twelve years old and really had never been interested in girls - until I saw you. Wow! I found myself waiting for you to come back on screen in every scene. I think I swam (floated) out of that theater just thinking of your blue eyes.

Beyond my first movie star crush, we all left that theater as a pretty happy family.

We had gotten to experience a great story together and we talked about it all the way home. It's a wonderful memory that I will cherish for as long as I live...

Parents have sacrificed so that their children could see the film.

A year after I first saw the film, we moved to a small town in northern Canada. I was six and The Sound of Music *came to town. Oh, but I wanted to go, so my mother brought me into the theater and sat me down and asked the manager to keep an eye on me. Mom didn't stay in the theater with me - she picked me up after the show.*

This was back in 1968. Only a few weeks ago, my mother told me the reason I sat through The Sound of Music *alone was because she and Dad couldn't afford to make it a family outing, but knew how much the film meant to me.*

I am now 37 going on 38, and this Christmas, Santa brought me a music box that plays "Edelweiss." Mothers never forget...

Of all the scenes in the movie, the moment when the Captain reaches out to his children is perhaps the single most beloved.

Fathers can relate to the story line in The Sound of Music, *especially in the scene where Christopher Plummer walks in and the children are singing, and as he joins in, he realizes what he has missed through the years. This scene is enough to 'jerk a tear'. Having two children of my own, the film made me realize how lucky I am to have such close relationships with them.*

That one scene in the film certainly strikes a chord in me regarding the relationship I have with my own father. I have heard from many people who wish they could have a resolution similar to the one the von Trapp children experience with the Captain. I envy those who succeed.

I can't tell you how many times I've seen The Sound of Music. *Of course, I always know what's coming and I know it's considered schmaltzy and manipulative. But when Captain von Trapp walks into the room and begins singing "The Sound of Music" with his children, I am moved almost to the point of tears every time.*

We all long to connect strongly in a special way to our fathers. My dad was a great father, but he became extremely busy in his work in education and ministry. I finally wrote him a letter about it when I had been college almost a year without hearing from him. He was in Germany at the time and his humble, loving response to my note was overwhelming. I wept openly. It was basically like the Captain walking back into that room, singing softly.

At that point, we began a wonderful relationship. He took great interest in everything I was doing. We even planned to start a creative communications studio together upon his retirement. Then, while riding his bike along a scenic path in Germany, my father was struck and killed by a tram.

I couldn't begin to tell you what it meant to me that he came back into "my room." It challenges me to stay connected with my own kids. Somehow, when it's "our turn" to do this for others, as we move from our own childhood to adulthood, we can lose sight of the responsibility (and opportunity) in the midst of our own ambitions, disappointments and wounds...

The film reflects people's deepest hopes and desires. As they grow older, the film becomes connected to memories of the time when they were young and at home with their parents.

Back in 1975, I was five years old and sick with the flu when my mom let me stay up to see The Sound of Music *on television. It was the first time I'd ever seen it and I tried so hard to stay awake! I remember the wedding scene, but nothing after it. I lapsed into semi-consciousness and had odd, fever induced dreams about shapes and songs for the remainder of the movie.*

I've seen it a million times since, and I'm always a little excited at the wedding scene because I know I'll get to see the film all the way to the end. But no matter how many times I watch it, the first time - even though I didn't see the whole thing - was the best, because we were all watching it together and my Mom and Dad made it something special. It's funny how the film seems to be a touchstone for so many people - and for so many different reasons...

She's right. The film is a touchstone for people because they grew up watching the video and listening to the soundtrack over and over.

The soundtrack from the movie was very present in my home growing up and hearing it brings back treasured memories of growing up in a house full of music and joy.

I was involved in theater as a child, and actually performed in The Sound of Music. *My first time was when I was twelve, and my mother was also in the cast, playing Sister Berthe.*

There is a picture in our family room of all the nuns from that production, and a close-up of my mother in profile in costume. When people ask about the pictures, I always say, "Oh, those are shots of my mother when she was a nun," which generally leaves them delightfully perplexed.

I'm always struck by the detailed memories some people have of seeing the film as children, and the way in which they pass on this gift to the next generation.

I remember watching the film for the first time when I was seven. It was nothing grand - just some M&M's and a blanket in front of my father's favorite chair. Little did I know then I was watching something that would become like a favorite friend.

I like to think that this movie continues to make friends even today. I teach second grade and I have shown the film each year I've taught (in fact, one of my more 'verbal' boys informed me last year that you were 'fine'.) I love watching my students get caught up in the storyline.

All of these things to simply say, thank you. The Sound of Music *has always brought me so much joy...*

The film is an integral part of many people's memories of how their family even began. Couples from around the world have written to share how the film is a part of their own beginnings. A woman from Israel told me of the love she and her husband have for the film, and of how he serenaded her with "Sixteen Going On Seventeen" on one of their first dates. They later played it at their wedding, and they feel it is 'their song'. The film, for her, represents the early beautiful days of friendship and courtship she and her husband shared.

It's wonderful that people, who have fond memories of watching the film during their childhood, then choose to pass the experience on to their own children.

My first memories of The Sound of Music *are from when I was six years old and my grandmother took me to see it. I was enthralled. My fondest memories of my grandmother (now almost 80 and still singing at church and playing her piano and singing in nursing homes) are of her pushing me on the swing set and singing "Do-Re-Mi."*

Recently, my two daughters, ages 10 and 8, were cast in a local production of the play. It brings tears to my eyes to watch them rehearsing and having so much fun, and knowing that this love for The Sound of Music *started with my grandmother...*

Another letter expressed a similar sentiment.

I first saw the film when I was ten and I was captivated by its beauty and magic, just totally entranced. I cried floods of tears when the Captain joined the children in song and when the family was climbing the mountain at the end. No other movie had or has the same emotional effect on me. It's heartwarming, inspiring, uplifting, poignant and romantic - a truly timeless classic.

I recently introduced my four-year-old twin daughters to my favorite video tape, and they were instantly immersed in it, wanting to watch it daily. Their favorite song is "So Long, Farewell" and they act it out, with one twin standing behind the other and popping out to say, "Cuckoo."

I am so happy my girls share the same love for The Sound of Music *that I have. Hence, a new generation of* Music *lovers is born!*

When people ask me why the film is so successful, I think one reason is that there's such a great age range in the characters, from little Gretl who's five to Liesl who's sixteen to the youthful Maria and the mature Captain and the Baroness and Uncle Max and the Reverend Mother. Sometimes, these characters become 'real people' for a family.

My family of eight kids and my parents (I'm 20, and we all go down in age from 18 to 14 to 12 to 11 to 9 to 7 to 5) tried to sing together a few times (like the von Trapps), but I don't sing well and my dad and 14 year old brother can't carry a tune, so help them. So we approached our music minister at our church about playing handbells instead of singing.

He was delighted to teach us. We started two years ago, and within months we had started calling our music minister "Uncle Max", and he was very much like that character. He had us going everywhere he could to play, and he loved showing us off.

We still call him Uncle Max, even though we've moved to a different state. God has now blessed us with four octaves of our own bells and we play everywhere we can, and everywhere we go, people look at us and say, "Oh, you're kind of like the von Trapps, aren't you?"

In *The Sound of Music*, there's someone and something for everyone to identify with, from the wide range of characters to the gorgeous scenery and the city of Salzburg. Sometimes the film has even helped people to find 'new families'.

The Sound of Music is my all time favorite movie. It is the reason I pursued a Masters Degree in German Language and Literature. I studied for two years in Salzburg and scouted out all the locales used in the movie. I lived just two blocks from Mirabel Gardens where I used to study and people watch. Thanks to Music, I learned a new language, lived in a beautiful city, and met people who started off as friends and are now my family...

The film can be powerfully connected to climactic family events.

The first time I saw the movie, I was living in Germany. I had no idea how The Sound of Music would be my lifeline in the years to come. To explain: I was born in Germany, and adopted by an American family when my adopted father was stationed in Germany in the mid-sixties.

In 1988, I opened my adoption records on the net and found my family in Germany. That December, I flew with my husband and daughter over to Germany to meet my four sisters and my father. My daughter practiced "Sixteen-Going-On-Seventeen" on her flute, and then she played it for the family, with me singing the song.

Ever since the day I found my family, I cry like a baby whenever I watch The Sound of Music. Thank you for the wonderful years of support and just being there for me, and for all the young girls hearts you have touched...

Sometimes the film simply reminds people of their own families.

I have loved The Sound of Music for most of my life. I've always been able to identify with the von Trapps in the movie because I'm from a large, female-dominated family (five sisters but unfortunately no brothers!), and my mom was actually a postulant in a convent before she married my dad.

Liesl always reminded me of my older sisters - pretty, and slightly rebellious, but essentially sweet and maternalistic towards us younger siblings. In short, she epitomized for me all the good qualities an older sister should have (and she could sing and dance!).

Or it literally reminds them of home.

Our home is a Swiss chalet located in the Wisconsin woods, built by our own hands. We have German geraniums in the window boxes on the balcony and a set of "Sound of Music" plates hang on a display shelf in the dining room.

My husband and I both came from German backgrounds and to me, The Sound of Music *reflects the heritage of both my family and my husband's family. I will never tire of seeing it.*

The film is something that parents and their children can enjoy together, always.

My wife and I periodically show the film at home and view it with our children. While they are now typical teenagers who try to avoid any movie made before 1985, they really enjoy watching it and sharing the beautiful story and music with their ancient, out-of-touch parents.

Thank you for your part in such a much-needed and always-appreciated movie that families can watch and enjoy together throughout the years...

I have heard that when teenage boys find it difficult to relate to their fathers, they can still talk about baseball. With mothers and teenage daughters, *Music* can break the ice the same way.

I have had a difficult relationship with my mother, but one of the things that we were always able to talk about was The Sound of Music.

Many college students have found the film to be an antidote for homesickness. A young woman told me how her family would watch the film together every year when it was on television, and how her father would always sing "Edelweiss" along with Christopher Plummer. When she went away to college, she turned on the television in her dorm one night and found that *The Sound of Music* was on. She realized it was the first time she wouldn't be able to watch it with her family and immediately called home to tell them that she was thinking of them.

She then settled in to watch the film by herself. And when the scene with "Edelweiss" came on, she cried, for she knew that back home, right at that exact moment, her father was singing along with Captain von Trapp.

Other college students have shared similar stories.

Your movie has been a constant in my life since I was very young. When I packed for college last year, I made sure that the video came with me to school. I can't describe the feeling that I get when I watch it. As I see the familiar scenes and listen to the family songs, feelings of warmth and love fill my soul. Even after watching the movie a ridiculous amount of times, I still cry EVERY SINGLE time I watch it.

Thank you for creating the most amazing movie ever made, and for giving me so much hope and life...

Of course, sometimes college students tell me things that make me cringe a bit.

I am a senior at Purdue University. Despite being poor college kids, my friend and I got the new DVD of the film yesterday (it was either pay the phone bill, buy groceries, or purchase The Sound of Music *on DVD and of course I had to choose the latter...)*

While I'm flattered that the film is so important to him, I happen to think the phone bill's important, too. Still, sustenance for the soul is essential.

The Sound of Music always made me feel safe and happy. Growing up, I went to bed with my t.v. on, and when I went away to college, I, of course, had my ever beloved copy of the film with me. I put the tape in the VCR and let Maria sing me to sleep. I was away from home, and, as usual, The Sound of Music *was there, making me feel safe.*

No movie in history ever had, or ever will have, an effect on my life that "Music" has. Thanks for changing my life - without even knowing it. You will always be forever Liesl to me...

Not only have college students brought it from home for solace, other people have taken it with them to the most interesting places. Like the delivery room.

I packed my copy of The Sound of Music *video in my suitcase when I went to the hospital to have my first son. I watched the entire first tape in between my childbirth breathing. After that, I needed to concentrate on the baby a little bit more...*

This isn't the only time I've heard about *The Sound of Music* being used as a lamaze coach.

I was working for the Dutch Embassy in Iran and was talking to a colleague there one day and suddenly we were discussing the births of our children and she said she had delivered both her boys while watching The Sound of Music. *I was so surprised! There she was, my no-nonsense colleague, telling me that through the hard work of delivering a child, she had actually enjoyed the story and the songs of the movie...*

Others just find that, wherever they are in life, *The Sound of Music* makes them feel like they are home.

I have always been close to my family and miss them horribly... but I have found that music, and The Sound of Music, *cross the distance and help me feel closer to home...*

Some letters I've received make me laugh out loud, like the one from a young woman who wrote to tell me that as a little girl, she wished Liesl was her big sister because growing up with three brothers was no piece of cake.

But other letters bring me to tears, and make me aware of the way in which this one movie has poignantly touched people's lives.

I had not thought much about the movie until recently, when I played the soundtrack on the car CD for my grandchildren, ages 8, 5 and 3. Little did I realize how much they would enjoy it. But the biggest surprise was my brother, age 63.

My brother was hit by a car when he was on active duty in the U.S. Army in Germany at the age of 26, and suffered permanent brain damage. Although he is independent, I am his caregiver.

That day, the children were sitting in the back seat, and my brother was sitting up front, beside me. You can imagine my shock when I looked at him and there were tears streaming down his face. Later, I asked him about it and he said he was thinking about the children in the movie. His tears were tears of happiness for the children because in spite of the war, their family had survived. He said the whole story made him happy, and it was hard for him to find the words to express that. As you once wrote, the movie and the songs reflect the emotions we already have. You're right.

He began to cry again, and said if he had the movie, he'd watch it right then. Ironically, my brother's birthday was the following day and one of the gifts he received was The Sound of Music...

This woman's story touched me deeply, and it meant a great deal to me to ultimately meet her and her brother at a book signing. Usually I'm not able to put a face on the fans who write to me, nor am I often able to truly express what their letters and stories have meant to me over the years. Perhaps, one person's letter helps me sum up my own feelings.

I just wanted you to know: you've been like family to me for most of my life.

So have all of you to me.

The Human Spirit

As we set off on a day of filming during the middle of our week here, our producer drove us out toward the location of one of the "von Trapp" houses used in the film. We stopped on the opposite shore of the lake from Leopoldskrön and looked back across the water at the villa where we filmed many of the scenes for *The Sound of Music.*

Hundreds have written to tell me of their visits to this site. Some have very special memories of their time on the shore of this lake.

I have been a fan from the first time I saw the movie. When I was nineteen, I spent a year hitchhiking and working in Europe with five friends in 1967. It was the first time any of us had ever been away from home for the holidays and we were all a little homesick.

We found ourselves in Salzburg over Christmas, and it snowed on Christmas Eve as we walked to midnight Mass at the cathedral in the center of town. The music was incredible. The town, as well as the fortress above, were all lit with white lights. It was an experience none of us will ever forget.

Christmas Day I hauled my friends all over Salzburg looking for places I remembered from the movie. We found the pond where you all fell out of the canoe, and took a picture of the six of us in front of the gate, with the pond behind us, singing our hearts out as we recreated that scene from the movie, acting like idiots, when we heard laughter coming out of the building in front of us (Leopoldskrön). It was full of American college students spending their junior year abroad and they invited us in for some Christmas cheer.

Needless to say, the movie made a lasting impression on me, and was part of a Christmas memory that none of us will ever forget...

There were actually two different houses which were used during the making of the film: Leopoldskrön on the lake, and Frohnburg, which doubled as both the front and back of the house. Neither was the actual villa where the Trapp family had lived, but still, the sight of our film 'von Trapp house' fills me with thoughts of the real von Trapps and of the beauty which they chose to give up by fleeing Hitler. I can't imagine what it would be like to suddenly uproot and leave my own home and all the memories that have been made there, all the friendships and familiar landmarks and comforts. It would not be easy to give up everything.

When we were filming here, Salzburg denizens were still uncomfortable with their Nazi history. In fact, assistant director George Steinitz remembers that the city refused to give its consent when Bob Wise wanted to film a scene with hundreds of Nazi troops marching into the central Plaza, with cheering Austrians welcoming them and swastika flags decorating the buildings. I don't know who then negotiated with the local politicians, but someone from Twentieth Century Fox gently suggested that if they weren't allowed to film, actual newsreel footage of the Anschluss would be used, showing the Austrian citizens waving and cheering the Nazi troops as they entered Salzburg in 1938.

A compromise was reached in which the scene was rewritten to occur several days after the Nazi arrival in Salzburg, with Nazi flags flying and troops marching across the plaza, but no cheering throngs of Austrian citizens. So the image of the Anschluss was downplayed slightly in the film, though it certainly was not avoided.

Of course, the story of the von Trapp family was also altered for dramatic purposes, with dates being compressed and the names and ages and the birth-order of the children being changed. The seven children were actually Rupert, Agathe, Maria, Werner, Hedwig, Johanna and Martina, and by the time of the Anschluss, the real Georg and Maria von Trapp had already been married for over ten years, and had two daughters of their own, Rosmarie and Eleonore (son Johannes was born in the United States in 1939).

I've always found the true story of the Trapp family as compelling as the somewhat fictionalized one we portray on screen. Theirs' is the story of seven adults choosing to leave their home, their country, their language and everyone that they knew, to accompany their father and step-mother and two little sisters on a journey into the unknown. There is something very American to me about the family's risky escape and their travel westward, surviving on faith while they sought their freedom.

I've only known members of the family for a short while and have been able to see them on just a handful of occasions, but when I am together with the six surviving von Trapp children, I'm filled with a sense of belonging. We have a unique relationship, as if we are distant cousins whose ties are not totally clear, but who are part of an extended family. We are bonded, not by blood, but by a story, their story, and the impact it has had upon the world, and while we haven't known each other for long, we've known *of* each other for decades.

My first meeting with them was so warm and loving, and the more I have gotten to know them, the more fond I have become of the family. They inspire me. They arrived in America with nothing in their pockets, yet have built an incredible home for themselves in Stowe, Vermont. They have brought music into millions of lives, not only through the play and the movie, but through their own music-making across the country, and in the meadows and hills surrounding their family lodge.

They invited the seven of us from the 'film family' to join them during a Trapp family reunion in Stowe, and while not all seven of us could make it, Debbie and Duane were able to come, and I brought along my youngest daughter, Emily, and her husband, Grant. From the moment I arrived, I felt I was among lifelong friends. There were hugs and laughter and such a welcome feeling that it seemed I was returning home after a long time away.

Agathe and Maria and I were like the three musketeers during my time in Stowe, and I reveled in getting to know them better. They have lived phenomenal lives, these von Trapp women, lives filled with self-sacrifice. Choosing not to marry, they became missionaries in distant corners of the planet, working hard to make others happy and spiritually enlightened.

Their land in Vermont reminds me a great deal of the hills in Austria, and on our first afternoon together, Emily and Grant and Debbie and Duane and I traipsed down to the amphitheater in the meadow and sat on the grass, having a picnic while we listened to a harpist play. We spent the entire afternoon sipping wine and talking under the Vermont sun and it felt as if we were in a distant magical kingdom. It was one of the most serene experiences I've ever had.

At dinner, Maria and Agathe wore their traditional Austrian dresses and we sang songs together and afterwards, Maria said, "I want you to see our real story." We all sat down with her to watch *Die Trapp Familie*.

This film, made by German director Wolfgang Reinhardt back in the 1950's, was the first dramatization of the Trapp family story, and it is different from *The Sound of Music*. The time frame is more accurate. In *Die Trapp Familie*, Georg and Maria marry in 1927, just as they did in real life, and their own children are born. But the reason they leave Austria is not depicted in any detail.

Since the film was in German, without subtitles, Maria translated the whole film for us in English. She was a fireball, narrating for us with great passion and animation. There she was, in her mid-eighties, ready to go the whole night and I was about ready to collapse. But it was such a special thing to share with us, and I was struck by her words. "Our real story."

The Trapp family's personal history has been fictionalized over the years. Many myths and 'enhanced truths' simply aren't true. Things have been written and accepted that have been a source of frustration, particularly about their father, who was a very kind and powerful man, who always kept music alive in their home. As *The Sound of Music* became known worldwide, they felt their father's memory was being unjustly rendered, and I think I would feel the same if he'd been my father. It is my hope that one day one of the original von Trapp children will write down their own version of the family story, so the world will know more about this wonderful man and his first wife, Agathe, without whom the Trapp Family Singers - and *The Sound of Music* - never would have existed.

One misty morning in Stowe, Emily and I walked a mile from the Lodge to the small cobblestone chapel that Werner von Trapp built with his own hands. It had rained, and the trees surrounding us were thick with the scent of newly washed leaves and stones. Inside the chapel, there was paper for writing and a small tray. If you wanted to ask the Lord a question or for help, you could write it down and leave it on the tray, and later, the family would pray for you. I did, and interestingly, the question I wrote down that day was answered.

I loved Stowe and the time I spent there with my extended family. I hated for our time there to end, to leave the von Trapps and the loving serene atmosphere of their home. I think others who visit there feel the same.

I saw the movie for the first time when I was ten. Everyone told me I would love it and I did. When our family went on a trip to Stowe, Vermont, we went to the von Trapp's lodge. We spent hours walking around the grounds and I was in awe when we saw Maria von Trapp tending a garden, dressed in traditional Austrian attire. My family loved the scenery and the special connection we felt to the film while we were there, and we returned to Stowe many times. This connection continued into my adult life when my husband surprised me with a trip to Stowe for my 30th birthday...

There *is* a very special feeling at the von Trapp's home. It is a godlike place which holds a special significance for many people.

When my wife and I were married, we asked that the "Processional" and "Alleluia" from The Sound of Music *be played during the ceremony. We then spent our honeymoon in New England, with the von Trapp Family Lodge as the grand finale. We met Johannes and attended a singalong with Rosmarie, and during one dinner, we leapt out of our seats because we heard songs from the musical coming from the lounge. Sure enough, a group of nuns were there, singing away! It turned out to be a group of performers from a local stage production...*

Members of the Trapp family stand as representatives for the thousands upon thousands of refugees who were uprooted during WWII. Their courageous stand against evil is, for many people, the heart of the film.

I first saw The Sound of Music *at age six with my twin brother and our older sister. I was so charmed by the wonderful story, the breath-taking scenery. I thought perhaps I'd outgrow my attachment to this film as I entered adulthood, but quite the contrary. This movie touches me more now than ever.*

As an adult, I'm able to appreciate even more about the story, including the profound implications of the sub-plot, the annexation of Austria by Nazi Germany. More than anything, I think The Sound of Music *is about the power of the human spirit to rise above all opposition...*

I couldn't agree more. While the film tells the story of love between Maria and the Captain, and the family love between the children and the adults, these emotions are heightened by the backdrop of the Anschluss, and the risk of standing up to that evil. The human spirit that the von Trapp family demonstrated in real life has inspired the world.

I saw The Sound of Music *at Radio City Music Hall in 1975. I was nineteen at the time, and at that point I understood and appreciated the film's themes. I was moved to tears more than once.*

You know, it was thirty years after the end of the war, and ten years after the film's original release, and the ENTIRE *audience broke into a rousing cheer, with sustained applause, when Christopher Plummer tore down the Nazi flag and destroyed it. What a powerful, moving film. It never fails to reaffirm my belief in the goodness of humanity...*

There's a story about filming that scene with the flag. During the first take, when Chris tried to pull it down, the flag was too well made and too well attached. He pulled and pulled and ended up swinging from it. The flag finally came down on the second take, and his vehemence in then tearing it in half has ignited audiences worldwide.

I received a letter which illustrated for me how differently a child could interpret that scene.

When I was very young, I didn't understand the political elements within the film and I remember asking my mother, "Why is the Captain ripping up that flag like that?" My mother was silent for a time, then she said, "There are some terrible things in the world, darling, and sometimes you do little things to make yourself feel better about them."

Still, I wondered why the Captain had to rip the flag down and tear it up. The movie was so glorious, he certainly didn't need to make himself feel better. To me, the film was set in a perfect world. It wasn't until I was older that I could understand the significance of that scene and the family's journey over the mountain at the very end of the film...

The film has inspired young people to contemplate the price of war.

I am fifteen years old and have been a huge fan of The Sound of Music *since I was three. When I was young, it was the music and the children's story that attracted me to it. But now that I'm older, and have studied World War II, I can really understand the emotional part of the movie. The story has helped me to see life for what it really is...*

A young woman echoes his comments.

In my history class, we started discussing the Anschluss and I took off. I spent the entire class talking about how "Rolf" epitomized the Aryan-youth and the movie's portrayal of the von Trapp's escape. For the first time, I realized how much The Sound of Music *had taught me. I had no idea how much about the history of modern Europe I knew just from watching a movie a hundred times...*

It has inspired others to understand more about the German culture.

After seeing the film as a teenager, I elected to study German instead of Spanish which most of my friends were taking. I gained an appreciation of the German and Austrian Teutonic culture, and understood the difference between Germans and Nazis at a time when most people in my community still looked upon anything German as evil and warlike.

Many people have written about when they saw the film back in the 60's and the film forced them to see, just twenty years after VE-Day, that not everything Germanic was ugly. After all, the Trapps were of Teutonic descent.

Teachers have used the film in their classrooms to help students develop an empathy for the individuals affected by WWII.

I teach 7ᵗʰ Grade Social Studies and I use The Sound of Music *in my classes in our unit for Europe, teaching the students about World War Two, the invasion of Austria by the Nazi's, and yes, the von Trapp family singers who sing their way to freedom. I teach in a 'Title 1' school. My students come from extremely poor, single-parent families, and are 'labeled', many being put in special ed classes early in their educational life. With a passion, I set out trying to discover the keys to their intellect and I found that many of them are visual learners, so I began to incorporate films into my curriculum.*

It is with this type of teaching that I bring The Sound of Music *into the classroom when we study WWII. The film helps me teach the 'why's' of Hitler, why he invaded Austria and surrounding countries, and what his plan was, worldwide. My group this year has had a hard time understanding why someone would kill another human being just because they're Jewish.*

The Sound of Music *helps me give my students a visual to connect with, and thus, learning takes place. They might not be able to read, but they are able to comprehend, to feel and to learn, not just about the characters and the story - but about themselves as well...*

Without firing a shot, *The Sound of Music* has taught many people about war. But for many people, the film is a poignant reminder of something they personally know well.

My husband was born in Germany during the War, in 1941, and left for America in 1950 with his mother and sister. There are many things in The Sound of Music *that bring him back to those difficult times. The movie has a gentle way of reminding us that these things must never happen again...*

The film has helped many people to understand how the war affected members of their own family.

My father was born in Austria and had to leave in 1936 when he was 15 years old. He was the leader of an anti-Hitler group at his school and word leaked out one night that he and a few other boys were going to be rounded up and shot the next morning. His mother put him on a train that night to escape. He ultimately ended up in New York City where he learned English and worked for US Intelligence.

He tried to tell my brothers and me about his childhood in Stainach near Salzburg, and about how, as the oldest son in his family, he had many responsibilities. Life had been hard during the Depression, even for reasonably well off families such as my father's. One winter, he had to dig in the frozen fields to find potatoes left over from the past summer's harvest.

My brothers and I viewed this story as another exaggeration from an out-of-touch old Austrian who was trying to get us to finish our dinner. My father was somewhat of an embarrassment to us, what with his accent and his bent for discipline from the old country. He was one of those "50's" dads who didn't show much emotion to his kids and 'ruled with an iron fist.' He wasn't easy to get close to. I didn't ask him questions about his past. My brothers and I assumed, as kids do, that he had no life before we were born. I really didn't know much about Austria or the Nazi's despite his stories.

When The Sound of Music *came out in 1965, we went to see it. I was eleven. The old adage 'a picture is worth a thousand words' is true. Watching the film, my father's own escape from the Nazi's became a lot more real to me, and helped me to understand him and his sometimes angry behavior.*

The scene in the movie in which the father sings "Edelweiss" to his children was especially moving. Up to that point in the film, Georg had a lot in common with my father. Disciplinarian, non-emotional, aloof. Seeing him suddenly change character was really something for me. That far-off look in Georg's eyes reminded me a lot of the far-off look my own father would get when telling his stories about Austria.

After seeing the movie, my father told me with excitement about seeing the very rare edelweiss on rock ledges and cracks high up in the mountains that he climbed as a boy. The movie caused me to ask him questions and allowed me to have more common ground to discuss things with him. I can't say he had the major reversal of character that Georg did, but he did seem less distant. Ultimately, the film helped give me a much better understanding of what he went through and why he was like he was.

He bought a "Sound of Music" story hard cover book that sat on our coffee table for years. It was the catalyst for occasional conversations. I particularly remember one we had about the photograph of Georg ripping down the Nazi flag at his house. It made me realize how I would hate to have someone come to my house and put up a Nazi flag and try to take over my country. It put me in my father's shoes.

My dad was very proud of his heritage and I know he was grateful for the opportunity The Sound of Music gave him to improve communications with me and to convey his love for his homeland. I learned about his Father, Mother, seven brothers and sister, (my grandparents, uncles, and aunt), most of whom were killed during the war. Happily, he tracked down his two surviving brothers thirty-three years after he left Austria. The story of their reunion made front page news in our local newspaper as well as the newspapers in the towns in Norway and France where my Dad's brothers were living.

In my post-teen years I overcame my embarrassment of my Dad and became proud of him. I don't know how he survived leaving home for good at age 15 to travel around the world and start a new life in a foreign country.

For Father's Day a year before my father died, my two young daughters, then aged three and four, sang "Edelweiss" to me, something my wife had taught them. Later, they sang it for my father. It was very special to me. It's my father's song...

Many of the stories people have shared with me make me acutely aware of the cost of the war, and the incredible gift of freedom we enjoy within our own borders in America.

My dad was born in 1940, on a German homesteaded farm in Poland. He was the fourth of five children. When the German's invaded Poland, his dad, my grandpa, Opa, was given a choice of fighting for the Nazi's or being killed on his front porch. Naturally, he chose to live and took his chances fighting on the side of a cause he didn't believe in. He was shot in battle, and shot the man who shot him. Thankfully, the bullet that hit my Opa was deflected from his heart by a wallet filled with family pictures. *(Ironically, many years later, when my dad's family moved to the States, he met that man that shot him, and who he shot, and they became best friends.)*

After he recuperated, Opa was sent back out on the front lines. This time he figured out a way to not fight for the Nazi's and still keep his family safe: he surrendered to the English and spent the rest of the war in an English POW camp (Where dad said Opa was treated well).

After the war ended, Opa returned home to find his family had survived, but my dad said, Opa was never the same. Before the war, he was kind and gentle man, but now, something had changed. In addition, when Opa returned home he found his farm had been confiscated by the Nazi's to use as a headquarters.

Now, they had a new enemy to escape: Communism. When the Iron Curtain came down, Dad's family barely managed to escape to West Germany, becoming refugees, and ultimately finding their way to the United States when my dad was seventeen.

The last scene of the film, when the Von Trapps travel over the mountains to freedom, has always been poignant for me because of what my dad and his family went through to reach freedom in the United States. I can barely get through that scene without crying...

The Trapp family's resilience of spirit is one of the most moving themes of the film. Even though we don't know what will happen to them as they cross the Alps to freedom, we are left with a sense of hope for their future because they have each other.

The Sound of Music has always been very special to me. Both my mother and father were born in the same village in Austria and lost everything because of the war. When they both immigrated to Cleveland in 1953, they met again and were married...

The film provides a window to the experiences of refugees and survivors, everywhere.

My aunt and uncle took me to The Sound of Music *after it had already been playing for a year at the same theater in Rochester, New York. I was eleven. The story has a special application to my uncle because, like the von Trapps, he escaped from Europe to come to America, fleeing the Hungarian communist reign in 1959 and coming to the US where he met and married my aunt...*

I believe what happened during the annexation of Austria in 1938 could happen anywhere. The story of the von Trapps is as relevant now as it was for the generation that lived through World War II.

I've just returned from Salzburg and wanted to write to let you know how important I think The Sound of Music *still is, even today. While wandering through the pristine tranquil Austrian countryside and listening to the regal church bells in the quaint villages, it's difficult for the average American to imagine the hatred and destruction that WWII brought.*

Can we, too, be swept away by evil ideologies and the charismatic, or will we think for ourselves, like the von Trapps, and stand for right? What would we risk for freedom of conscience?

The Sound of Music *should be a major wake-up call to all of us...*

The Trapps view themselves as a family, not much different from any other, but I stand in awe of their triumph and of their strength of character.

On March 2, 2000, I flew to New York to attend an event hosted by the Austrian government at the Waldorf Astoria Hotel. The date marked the 35th anniversary of the premiere of *The Sound of Music*, and honored guests included Florence Henderson, who played Maria von Trapp on the Broadway stage long before she became Carol Brady, the Vienna Boys Choir, the Salzburg Marionette Players, Ted Chapin and Bert Fink of the

Rodgers and Hammerstein Organization, and two of my favorite people: Johannes and Maria von Trapp.

It was so good to see them, and especially to share this anniversary with them. As the evening program began, they were called to the stage, where they sang for us, something they have done as a family for most of their lives. And then, they extended a hand to me and invited me to join them. The three of us paid homage to the film that links us to each other: we sang "Edelweiss".

There, on that stage, I felt something I'd never felt before. I was a member of The Trapp Family Singers. It was one of the nicest feelings I've ever had.

The Children

When Judith, our producer, asks the seven of us if we'd be willing to do the finale of "Do-Re-Mi" on the Salzburg steps of Mirabel Gardens, I am sure everyone will say, "No way." But my film siblings jump up like children to do it.

The director has a laptop computer with a DVD copy of *The Sound of Music* on it, so we first watch our moves in the movie, then race to the steps and try to recreate them. When Nicky says, 'Let's rehearse this a few more times," I almost fall over because I know how having to recreate any dance steps from the film is his biggest nightmare. He's a tremendous actor and writer, but dancing is just not his thing. I stare at him for a moment and when he grins I realize: he is enjoying this. And, ever the professional, he wants it to be good.

Then the jokes start. "Well, finally," Kym says, "after all these years being the youngest is an advantage." She easily mimics 'Gretl's' simple moves, hopping up the steps one at a time.

"Unfair!" Heather and I growl.

Since we were the oldest in 1964, and were dancers, we have the most intricate moves. I'm *still* the oldest, by a lot, and I've had knee surgery and haven't jumped down a flight of stone steps in decades. "I'm a grandmother!" I protest, but Kym only grins wickedly as she watches me navigate the steps, backwards.

For a moment, we truly are children again. Everything is exactly as it was back in 1964. The same people aren't listening to the director and following instructions, the same people are giggling. Nothing has changed, except that we're all thirty-five years older.

A crowd of tourists begins to gather and we can see the disconcerted looks on their faces, as if they aren't sure they're actually seeing what they're seeing. This can't really be those von Trapp actors, now middle-aged, hopping up and down on these steps. Our director finally has the cameraman pan our 'audience' standing their with their jaws open watching the seven of us hopping around like children.

Looking beyond the crowd, I'm struck by how small everything is. All seven of us have the same reaction. The steps of Mirabel Gardens and all the statues and fountains seemed much bigger back in 1964.

I can understand how Kym and Debbie might feel that way, since they were only five and seven when we last here. I'd expect their perspective would be different, a child's perspective. But I feel the same way, too, not only here, but at every location we visit, and I was twenty-one. Why do I remember all these places as so big and expansive? Perhaps I, too, saw them from a child's perspective back then.

Children see things differently. I love when they write to me because they always tell me exactly how they feel and what they think.

Dear Liesl,

I am five going on six. We all love to watch and listen to The Sound of Music *on record and on video. Daddy thinks that you still look lovely!*

It's always nice to know parents think I still look lovely! When children meet me in person, they expect to see Liesl, not a grandmother. They stare at me, confused, and won't believe I'm Liesl until after I sing to them. They want to meet Liesl, not Charmian Carr.

Dear Liesl,

I am 7 years old. I love watching The Sound of Music. *Mummy said you hurt your ankle when you filmed that dance. Have you ever come to Australia? That is where I live. How old are you now? I hope you don't mind me asking you lots of things. I have to go. I think you are very special...*

I think the children that love *The Sound of Music* are very special, too.

I am 12 years old and you are one of my favorite people in the whole world. I know the movie in German and English by heart because I go to Austria every summer. All my friends and family call me Liesl. I love dark chocolate too.

Love, Liesl II

Anyone who is a fan of dark chocolate is a friend of mine. Time to start yet another club. We'll have the Liesl Club, the Rolf Club, and the Dark Chocolate Club, though I fear I might be denied membership for I am not a purist: it's dark chocolate with almonds that I truly love.

Children of all ages write me about their desire to play a von Trapp.

Dear Charmian Carr,

I am thirteen years old and I love to watch the movie over and over. I have always wanted to play Liesl or Louisa, my favorite roles. Please know I'm a big fan of yours...

The von Trapp children are wonderful characters to play. They are spirited yet talented, and capable of executing practical jokes while singing their way into anyone's hearts. Parents from all over the world have written to tell me how much their children love the characters and the music.

While many two-year-olds need to listen to Barney, my son always asks for 'the kids' CD when we are driving. I have been singing "Edelweiss" to him as a lullaby since he was a baby, and knew he was a true fan when I overheard him singing the part of "Do-Re-Mi" that starts, "When you know the notes to sing..."

He likes to spin "Like Maria" and has seen the movie tons of times, and in true two-year-old fashion, he wants me to turn off the film when it gets to the Laendler - since it's my favorite part...

Watching the film with their young children has created many wonderful memories for fathers.

I dusted off - rather my twenty-seven month old son dusted off - the "Sound of Music" video I bought several years ago (my first video purchase). He wanted to watch it.

The last time I'd viewed it was when he was an infant and very cranky. I put in the tape and then held him and rocked him and danced though the entire film, trying to keep him asleep while my wife tried to get some sleep herself.

Zoom ahead two years later and my young son and I are watching it together again - and loving it!

I love the vision of this father and son bonding over the film. More than one parent has found the film and the music helpful in getting their children to sleep.

My husband and I had special songs we'd sing to our four children when they were babies. My youngest son's was to the tune of "Edelweiss". His name is Robby Moss, so we'd sing, "Robby Moss, Robby Moss, every morning you greet me..." to the entire tune. This soothed our young son to sleep.

The first time we watched the film with our children, their eyes lit up when "Edelweiss" came on, and they yelled with excitement, "Robby! That's your song!"

Thank you from my heart for memories relived...

The film and the songs have a calming effect on very young children, as evidenced in this letter from a woman in Australia.

When our first child was eight months old, I put the video on one day and was surprised that he immediately settled and lay there on the floor transfixed to the TV. That became the pattern for us and every day, when he was unsettled, we would put him in his swing in front of the TV and he would watch The Sound of Music *all the way through, and usually fell asleep. As he became older, he still loved it, and up till he was around three, we would see it at least once a day.*

Now, eight years and three children later, it is still a family favourite. In fact, we have worn two copies of the video out and are now working on a third.

Very small children love the film, and act out scenes.

I have two-and-a-half year old boy/girl twins who have seen The Sound of Music *no less than twenty times! It's their favorite. They're mesmerized with the kids and the singing, and they've taken to dancing and swirling like Maria does on the mountain. It is so adorable. They know all the words to every song on the soundtrack. Of course, they should - they listen to it in the car all the time!*

Sometimes, parents have found their children mimicking lines from the film, to their own chagrin.

Yesterday I did something clumsy, and suddenly I hear my seven-year-old son mumbling, "Mummy is forty, going on forty-one, she should know what to dooooo," to the tune of "Sixteen Going on Seventeen"...

In one of my favorite letters, a mother made me laugh out loud.

My four-year-old son dresses up like a nun and sings "How do you solve a problem like Maria" all the time. We try not to worry about it...

Children develop make-believe relationships with the family they see on the screen.

My three-year-old has been watching The Sound of Music *for the past year and loves it. She knows the whole thing by heart, and she has a doll named Marta, and two of her best "make believe" friends are Rolf and Liesl...*

Teenagers and adults have written to tell me how they remember that the von Trapp children were their own imaginary friends when they were very young.

By the time I was three, I distinctly remember spending hour after hour, day after day, mesmerized by the scenery and songs of The Sound of Music. *By the time I was four, I would pick out a character at the beginning of the movie (usually Gretl) and pretend that I was her as I watched the movie, saying all her lines, singing all her parts.*

I developed imaginary friends, as do many pre-schoolers. Mine were the seven von Trapp children. I would walk around our house talking to and playing with Brigitta and Friedrich and Marta and all the rest. My parents thought I was crazy, but it seemed the most natural thing in the world to me. I knew all the songs and all the dances and wanted more than anything to be a part of that family. When people asked me what I wanted to be when I grew up, I would answer, "A von Trapp."

Eventually the imaginary friends went away as school started - but my love for the movie has never left me.

Around the world, children have been raised with this film as an on-going influence in their homes.

My father was from a small town near Banbridge, Ireland, where your father's family came from, and so I feel I have a small connection with you. When I was a kid of about six or seven years old, I watched The Sound of Music *every day, I'd guess close to a hundred times. My sister used to come down saying, "Are you watching that again?" I think she wanted to kill me.*

I knew every word and every song, and I would act it out. I really thought I was one of the von Trapps.

Some people can vividly remember how specific moments in the film affected them as children.

I can remember the first time I saw the movie, I was sitting with my parents, and when the cemetery scene came on I was certain that the family was going to get caught. I leaned from side to side with each of you as you tried to stay out of the way of the flashlight, and held my breath through the entire scene. I just watched the movie again the other day and found myself doing the same thing!

The cemetery scene is quite powerful to children. Another woman recounted almost exactly the same reaction.

Despite having seen the movie so many times, I always find myself holding my breath when Rolf finds you in the cemetery and my heart skips a beat as I find myself praying that you will get away.

Others remember how the film became part of a friendship.

I have warm memories of The Sound of Music *throughout my childhood. My best friend and I saw the movie when we were six, and ever after that we used to sing, "I am Six going on Seven." We were thrilled when we turned sixteen and we were finally as old as Liesl. The film will always be something that we come back to as a fun and special part of our childhood.*

People can remember the tiniest details, like the way in which they interpreted lines from the film's songs when they were children.

I first saw the movie when I was five in 1966, and I kept singing "tea, you drink with German bread". I know better now...

The strength of their memories fascinates me, recalling incidents involving the film or the soundtrack from very early childhood.

You are a part of my earliest memories. I was three or four years old and my favorite record was "The Sound of Music." That album dominated my childhood. My mother would sit me on the couch with a spoonful of peanut butter for a treat and I would sit and listen to the record, looking at all the pictures in the album. One day, I was to go to a friend's house to play, but I wanted to listen to my record. So my mother put the record in my hand and told me to have my friend's mother play it for me and off I went.

When I asked my friend's mother to play it, she pulled out her own copy of the album and put it on for me. I was so surprised to discover she had her own copy of the album. I really thought I owned the only copy of "The Sound of Music."

Others remember how the film reigned over certain periods of their childhood.

When I was eight, my parents and aunt and uncle went to Europe on a vacation, and my brother and I, along with our cousins, stayed with our grandparents for the month they were gone. My cousin and I passed our days watching The Sound of Music, *sometimes more than once a day. We got up in the morning, had breakfast, and put in the tape. When it was over, we'd rewind it and watch it again and again, day after day, week after week. We absolutely loved it.*

We quickly knew every line, every song, and picked out who we wanted to 'be'. Our favorite scene was at the party, when the children sing "So Long, Farewell" to the guests. We set up our grandparents' living room so we had 'steps' (the foot stool along with pillows at different heights) and my cousin would play Gretl, sliding herself up the steps backward, singing as she fell asleep. I would then go pick her up in my arms, just like Liesl did in the movie.

I can't express how much I love the movie or how wonderful those days were.

Teachers have let me know how much they enjoy using the music in their classrooms.

My husband and I teach the youngest children's choir at our church (4-6 year olds) and we follow the routine we learned from his mother, who continued the tradition she learned from her own father. She incorporated "Do-Re-Mi" as her warm-up song right after the film was released, and we do the same. Invariably, when we start with a new class, we see shyness and timidity dissolve from the faces of children who may have never sung with a group before as we launch into that familiar and beautifully joyful song. It may not be a religious song, but when asked why we sing it, one of the children replied, "Because it makes your voice go up and down all over, and it makes you feel all warm inside, and doesn't God do that?"

Another said, "And you can't stay mad at anyone when you're singing it either." (This after she and another child had a shoving match just before we began.)

Thank you for contributing so delightfully to a film which inspires smiles and songs for so many of us who love them.

And every once in a while, I hear a special story about how the film has been a catalyst for healing and bonding between a parent and child.

Three years ago my husband and I adopted two children who had been in foster care. One, a beautiful little girl, had led a terrible life.

My mother was born and raised in Salzburg and so I grew up with The Sound of Music. *Since I was a small child, I have been going to Austria and have always been in love with the film. I didn't think my daughter, after coming into my life when she was seven, would share this love. Not so.*

Charmian, she watches this film at least once a week. This movie, to her, is a 'dream'. Thank you for making a dream for my daughter. I am taking her to Salzburg this coming summer and it is all she can think about, seeing the places where The Sound of Music *took place.*

Bless you for bringing this movie into our lives. You are an angel.

I can only imagine how much that dream will come true for both of them on the streets of this city and the surrounding hills. Salzburg is a magical place.

As we finish our middle-aged remake of the "Do-Re-Mi" grand finale, and no one has broken their ankle or twisted their knee, I look at my second family laughing around me and it isn't hard for me to see them all as they were in 1964 when they were young.

Back then, I was immediately attracted to Kym because she was the youngest and I was the oldest. I had the position of taking care of her on the set and she was quite a character. She loved me. "You are so cute," she'd say, talking to me as if I was a little girl and she was a forty-year-old. She was always telling me how much she liked my dimples, and I thought she was just hysterical. I felt very protective of her, and in some ways was closer to Kymmie than any of the other children. I really felt like I *was* her big sister on the set. And I think she felt like she was my mother...

Of course, I was extremely fond of Nicky and grew quite close to him as time went on, but during the filming, he certainly didn't need anyone to look after him. He was a total professional, as was Angela, a veteran actress.

Angela and Heather were quite a pair. In love with the Beatles, always speaking in their special coded language, there were times when I envied them and their private world, and I've always admired the way they've remained best friends throughout the years.

Debbie was just a beautiful child. When she began to lose her teeth,

I felt so badly for her. Most children who are seven just have to worry about whether the tooth fairy will come. Debbie had to worry about dentists and articulating lines of dialogue with unfamiliar false teeth. She was a trooper.

Duane was very adventurous, very independent, and had so much energy. I remember how hard it was for him to sit still when we had to stand around and wait between shots. He wanted to be on the move, and I could relate to his level of energy. I liked being kept busy, and I was when we were in Salzburg. I never got to be with the kids for all their fun off the set in 1964, not even for a meal.

I'm making up for lost time now. And, if our experience jumping on the Mirabel steps is any indication, this time in Salzburg, I'm just one of the kids.

Friends Around the World

As we sit on the "Sound of Music" tour bus outside Salzburg, the fifty tourists on board the bus with us handle our presence with surprising nonchalance, as if they think the seven of us are a part of the tour every day. I'd heard about 'the tour' for years, and was glad to have a chance to see it. From what I'd been told, there were a few 'facts' I needed to set straight. For example, one woman wrote me after hearing about my book.

Dear Charmian,

I have been to Salzburg twice, and one time, the guide on The Sound of Music *tour told me and my friend that you were dead from a successful suicide attempt! So, as much as I am enjoying your book, I am also thrilled by it's mere existence because it means you are safe and that the tour guide was an idiot.*

I am happy to report that I am alive and well!

In the first years after the film was released, a handful of people visited Salzburg and tried to find the sites where we made the film, many all on their own. But in recent years, busloads of "Music" tours run non-stop every day, all day long.

I just went on the "Sound of Music" tour in Salzburg and I couldn't believe the number of people. At every film location, there are lines of tour buses full of people who want to see where the movie was shot. As soon as one bus pulls out, another takes it's place!

Of all the tourists who visit Salzburg, birthplace of Mozart and home to one of the greatest music festivals in the world, seventy percent come simply to see the locations where *The Sound of Music* was filmed, flocking from every corner of the globe to visit these sites as if they were shrines.

In 1970, I met and fell in love with my wonderful German wife of 30 years. During our honeymoon, we visited Salzburg and most of the spots seen in the movie. At that time, no one we met knew what we were talking about when we asked about The Sound of Music *movie sites (I understand there are now bus tours). The cemetery scene always bugged me because we couldn't find one in Salzburg that looked remotely like it. After reading your book I now know it had been in Los Angeles all this time...*

On our last European trip, we stayed in Austria. When we hiked up the mountain trail near our romantic hotel, my wife and daughter and I found a wonderfully large green meadow at the top. Wow, what a view! I couldn't help myself, but burst out in song with "I go to the Hills."

There is a reason why the seven of us are on this bus today: the tour is being discussed in the documentary we are making. The crew films us on the bus as we approach one of the locations, but there is a glitch and the director hasn't gotten the shot he wants. So the bus turns around and we go back and drive down the road again. There is yet another glitch, and back we go again for a third run, causing several of the tourists on board to groan in exasperation. Retakes are the bane of film-making and we try to make light of it, but I hear later that one of our fellow tour bus riders asked for his money back.

The "Sound of Music" tour is offered in at least eight different languages, and I am astounded by the numbers of people we see at the different locations. It is late fall, and I cannot fathom what the summer months must be like. But I shouldn't be surprised. For my entire adult life, I have witnessed, first hand, the fascination and love people have for the film, world-wide. Beginning in 1965, I traveled to dozens of countries as an ambassador for Twentieth Century Fox and everywhere I went, the reaction was the same: people around the planet adore *The Sound of Music*.

Their love for it has never ceased, and the studio has continued to keep me on the road over the years when they've released the soundtrack and the film on video and CD and DVD. My 'ambassadorship' appears to be a lifelong appointment. Just two years ago, I was sent to Australia to promote Fox's re-release of the video there. Nicky and I traveled from Sydney to Melbourne together, and couldn't get over the number of fans that turned out. One man drove six hours from his ranch in the Outback just to meet us, and once he shook our hands, he got back in his truck for the six hour drive back home.

Thousands came just to tell us, "Thank you." We were overwhelmed that, thirty plus years after *The Sound of Music's* premiere, people still felt so moved by it that they felt a need to express their gratitude for it.

The story and the music speak a universal language. I went to Japan last year, again at the behest of Fox, and my daughter Emily came along. Neither of my daughters had been exposed to 'the phenomenon' very much when they were growing up, and so for Emily, Japan was an eye-opener. The Japanese are crazy about the film.

I'm writing this from far away in Japan. The Sound of Music is, undoubtably, very famous here. We all grew up singing along with "Do-Re-Mi" an all other memorable songs. Music has no borders. I was about seven when I first watched it. Now seventeen years have passed since then, and it still captures my heart. It's just like magic. My impression of this film was so vivid that I can still remember how it was like to see it the first time. This sweet, heart-warming film showed me the power of song and family love. This film is truly timeless, the never-ending story which I cannot wait to share with my own kids in the future.

People in Japan turned out in droves. One woman I met heard that I was a new grandmother and made me three special origami figures: a mother, father and child, and presented them to me to give to my granddaughter, saying, "These will give her good spirit for marriage." (Now, a year later, here in Salzburg another woman also brings me a little doll she has made for me by hand. It turns out that her daughter was my 'stand-in' on the set in Austria and married Dan Truhitte. So not only do I have friends around the world - I have dolls from around the world...)

Everywhere Emily and I went in Japan, people were so gracious and generous, and clamored to get their picture taken with "Liesl." When it was time for me to go, everywhere I looked, people were crying.

It has been like this for over thirty-five years. The Trapp family's story seems to touch everyone, everywhere. Love, marriage, family, and honor, not to mention beautiful music and natural beauty, are things that translate into any language and cross every cultural barrier. *The Sound of Music* even has the power to reach beyond an Iron Curtain.

I grew up in Romania. During the 1970's, when we were under the terrible oppression of Ceausescu's iron rule, he tried to create an image of being more "western friendly." It was just an illusion, but along with it came an influx of American movies. These films changed our lives, particularly The Sound of Music.

There was little in the world of entertainment that made a real difference in our lives. Then "Music" opened and nothing was the same after that. My friends and I used to go see the movie over and over, year after year - more times than I dare admit to! I even learned English just watching, listening, and reading the subtitles.

It played in other Eastern Block countries as well. My father traveled to Poland when the movie opened there and he told me how people lined up for hours to see it.

To an entire generation in Eastern Europe, The Sound of Music *became an integral part of our lives. It brought so much joy to people, and for some of us, it crossed the line from being a form of entertainment to being a part of our lives. The actors and producers may never know us, but they touched us forever. And while you may not be aware of it, you are, in a way, part of our families...*

I have always known that the film is beloved internationally, but I never realized until quite recently that the film found its way past locked borders to brighten so many lives.

My name is Yelena. I'm 19 (going on 20) and a huge fan of The Sound of Music. *First time I watched it back when I was thirteen, I lived in Russia. I loved this film so much!!!*

The film has been shown in over two dozen languages, in every corner of the globe.

I am from India, and The Sound of Music *was one of the first films I ever saw, back in the days when communication was nowhere near as global as it is now. So you can imagine how great an impact the film had when I saw it, and loved it, in India as a little girl...*

Just like in America, people from every country can be reminded of time spent with their parents when they watch the film.

I am from Denmark, and The Sound of Music *was one of the first films my parents took me to, so I guess that's one of the reasons why its so special to me. Thank you for being part of that experience...*

It's part of people's childhoods and family memories, everywhere.

I'm from Ecuador, South America and I'm 26 years old. I first watched the movie when I was five, and it was love at first sight. That movie really touched me. The love, the songs, the characters; everything was perfect. I have a big family, two brothers and four sisters, and we all grew up with that beautiful story and its great songs. I just want to thank you and Julie, Christopher, Nicholas, Heather, Duane,

Angela, Debbie and Kym, for helping make people a little happier, and for teaching us that love breaks down all barriers...

It has been a calming influence on children the world over.

I live in Israel and I'm 17 years old. I was three when I first saw The Sound of Music *at my mom's friend's house. They needed something to keep me quiet with. I watched the film three times that day and didn't want to leave until my mom's friend agreed to give me the tape.*

I didn't understand English so it was hard at the beginning to figure what was going on. Eventually, I learned English through the movie. I have to say it is my favorite movie in the whole world. I know it by heart...

In every hemisphere, people have fallen in love with it.

I'm writing from Australia. I guess you've heard all this before, for everyone seems to have a "Sound of Music" story, or wants to tell you about their feelings and memories. But I wanted you to know the fact that, as many other people do, I know all the words to all the songs and love the movie. I used to dream I was in it...

They write to tell me of their love of the film, of the music.

I am from the Phillippine Islands. My family and I never tire of watching The Sound of Music *and hearing the songs. In fact, we memorized all of them!*

The film is a wonderful fantasy people around the world wish they could be a part of, as another woman in The Phillippines makes clear.

It has always been my dream to someday experience, however small, a little taste of what you portrayed on screen. That is the joy and youth that you so beautifully gave me in The Sound of Music. *My husband and I want to name one of our children Liesl...*

Friends around the globe don't just watch it once, but often.

I'm from Mexico and I like very very much the film. I have seen it a dozen times, and every time, is like the first time...

Once grown, people share this childhood favorite with their own children.

I write from Argentina where I live. The movie arrived in 1967 and I remember that the movie theaters showed it for two years. I saw it then, many times at the movies, and now I'm happy to see it whenever I wish with my three little daughters thanks to the VHS.

The film's meaning changes for people as they grow older, touching them on one level as a child, then as a teenager, then evoking other feelings in adulthood.

I am from Jakarta. I first watched The Sound of Music *in a cinema in Singapore in 1966 when I was ten. My father later bought the long-playing soundtrack for the family to keep the memory of the movie alive.*

The film had a more significant impact on me during my teens. I could relate to the relationship between Liesl and Rolf because I, too, at the time, was falling in and out of love. The film so inspired me that I wanted to find out what happened to the von Trapps after they had crossed the Alps. I sought out and managed to find both of Maria von Trapp's books about her and her family.

Now a father, with four children of my own, I'm still thrilled by the movie, and I can relate to the Captain's dilemma with seven children. It's funny how one's perspective and feelings for the movie change with age and time, but one thing has not changed - it has always remained a movie that I love and cherish.

The *Sound of Music* has encouraged people, worldwide, to empathize with the plight of those torn asunder by war and aggression.

I am a scientist in Japan. I first saw the movie in 1975, in a revival release, with Japanese subtitles. I was very moved by it.

No matter to what extent the story is based upon the true story, I felt that war drives many people into sadness. The splitting up of people who had been friends, or even family, such kind of sacrifice moved me.

I have a friend who hosted me when I did my post-doc in the United States. He was born in Germany, but his father hated the Nazi's, and so his whole family defected to the U.S. After the war, he went back to Germany. I thought how disastrous leaving his home, all his things, must have been, and how disastrous it also must have been to see his hometown after the war.

The von Trapps leaving home saddened me so much. "Climb Ev'ry Mountain," makes me cry. I even have tears writing this...

The "Sound of Music" fans in the United Kingdom are legendary, so I was glad when <u>Forever Liesl</u> gave me an opportunity to visit. Although my book tour there only gave me three days in London, I was delighted by the reception and the kindness I was shown, everything from the dark chocolate cake my publisher made for me, to the rollicking performance of the London "Singalonga" I attended, to the Internet fans who drove hours to come to my booksigning. Apparently, I am smaller in person than on the big screen.

You have no idea how much it meant to us to meet 'Liesl'. When you arrived at Selfridges, you were smaller than we expected, and a little older, obviously... But then you smiled at us and said, "Hi", and when we saw your blue eyes and heard that beautiful voice, we knew it was our Liesl standing before us...

From the British Isles to the tip of South America, from Alaska to Singapore and Tasmania to Egypt, people from every continent have let me know what *The Sound of Music* means to them.

I am from Argentina (at the bottom of America map). In Argentina, we are many "Sound of Music" fanatics. "Sound", for me, is the most beautiful movie and I guess it has made happy to millions across the wide Earth.

I want to tell you something rare happened to me. I studied Neuro Linguistic Programming techniques to improve communications at our company. There was an exercise where we had to tell about a story or a movie that had touched us deeply in our childhood. Half of the forty some odd people said, "The Sound of Music." Of course, I was IN the group.

The teacher said afterwards that the movie we had chosen had to do with our fantasies and the actual life we had had.

It has touched more hearts and souls than perhaps any other film.

My "Music"... It was my favorite thing when I was a little kid. It was even better than chocolate. And it is still my favorite thing in my adulthood - and it's still better than chocolate.

Sometimes I was Maria who was in love with the Captain, sometimes I was Liesl who had that romantic dance with Rolf in the gazebo, and sometimes I was little Gretl who dropped the tomato in the marketplace with the fear on her face. I was every character in the movie. It became part of my life and the best thing is - it still is. I can't stop my tears when I watch the movie.

A Forever Turkish "Sound of Music" Fan

The Sound of Music has left an imprint on every culture and every generation since it was first released, and I have every reason to believe it will continue to do so. To hear from so many people far and wide about it's unending impact inspires such hope in me. Although the film has always been criticized for being too sugary, it appeals to our better angels, and to me, the way in which the world has embraced it suggests that deep within us, we all cherish the same things: love, family, honor and integrity.

Long before the Internet made the world a smaller place, *The Sound of Music* spoke to the world. And the world responded to the music.

Singalonga

Here in Salzburg, everyone wants to know, "What do you think of this 'Singlalonga' thing?"

Members of our British film crew have seen it, but my 'film siblings' have not. "Is it something I could take my kids too?" Debbie asks.

"As long as they're wrapped up in brown paper and tied up with string." I grin at her perplexed look.

Singalonga Sound of Music is difficult to describe. You've got to see it to believe it. Part "Rocky Horror Picture Show", part karaoke, I didn't really 'get it' until I witnessed it first hand. That's when I became a *Singalong* fanatic myself.

I have just seen the 'Singalonga' in New York. What is your take on it? Do you think it's totally irreverent?

Yes, it's absolutely totally irreverent, and I love it! I wish I could take Chris Plummer. It would appeal to his sense of humor. When we were filming *The Sound of Music*, he went out of his way to play at the absurd, to infuse the set with his wicked wit. He liked to have fun, and fun is what *Singalonga* is all about.

It began in London as just a one night show at the London Gay and Lesbian Film Festival. An old print of the film was superimposed with the lyrics from the songs and the audience sang along with the characters on the screen. But that was only part of it. Audience members came dressed in costume, as Nazi's and nuns and Maria and the children, and overnight, *Singalonga* was born.

The inspiration for it came from an old age home in Inverness, Scotland. One of the therapists there had the residents singing along to videos of famous musicals to get them to be more active and social. A film festival organizer happened to be visiting his grandmother and, as he watched her singing along to *Seven Brides for Seven Brothers,* he thought, "We could do something like this at the festival."

And so they did. The original single showing turned into an encore performance, and now two years later, it's still selling out. I think no one believed that it would go on and on, but *The Sound of Music* is like that: it surprises people with its longevity.

I first heard about *Singalonga* from Ted Chapin and Bert Fink at the Rodgers and Hammerstein Organization. They had gone to one of the sellout shows in London, and they told me, "It's marvelous!"

With so many audience members coming in costume, a nightly contest evolved, and the night Ted and Bert attended in London, three men won who had come dressed as the Alps, with shaving cream on top their heads to add a nice finishing touch of snow. "You've got to see this, Charmy," Bert said. "It's hysterical."

I was intrigued, and a few months later, when I got a call from a group organizing an AIDS benefit in Austin, Texas, asking if I'd be willing to come to an event they were planning which was similar to the London *Singalonga*, I jumped at the chance.

I never anticipated how much the event would affect me. At the reception before the show, hundreds of costumed fans gathered around to tell me how much joy the film had given them throughout their lives. Their costumes were incredible, everything from men dressed as nuns to a woman who was a wild goose with a moon on her wings to a man dressed as a needle pulling a giant spool of thread.

Inside the theater, I couldn't get over the size of the crowd. Thirteen hundred people crammed into the Paramount Theater in Austin that night, spilling out of the seats and into the aisles. When the lights dimmed, the audience roared with excitement, and from the moment the opening scenes of the Austrian countryside appeared on that screen, I was caught up in the joy and enthusiasm that filled the theater. When Maria forgets her whimper on the hillside, someone in the audience shouted, "Maria! Your hat! Don't forget your hat!", and everyone started calling to her, "Your hat! Your hat!" until 'Maria' remembers and races back up the hill to retrieve it amid the cheers.

Such antics went on throughout the film, with people booing the Nazi's and cheering Maria, eating Captain Crunch cereal (provided in a goody bag that comes with the price of admission) when Chris Plummer says, "You may call me Captain", hissing at the Baroness and barking at Rolf ("Rolf, rolf, rolf!"). I'd never seen anything like it and I've never had so much fun.

If you had told me a quarter century ago that people would be dressing up in costumes in the year 2000 to come see *The Sound of Music* and sing lustily along with the songs on screen, virtually participating with the characters, waving Edelweiss and shooting off poppers when the Captain kisses Maria, I would have said you were crazy. But *Singalonga* isn't crazy at all. It's a wonderfully delicious event, born of infectious fun.

I believe *Singalong* (it's called 'Singalonga' in the U.K. and 'Singalong' in the U.S.) fulfills a basic human need. We humans need to congregate, to join together, to sing and to laugh out loud together. Opportunities to do that are sorely missing from our high-tech insulated lives. The silliness of *Singalong* might not be considered chic, but it's good for the soul, opening the door for grown-ups and children alike to play, to be gazebo dancers, if only for a few hours.

Yes, there are men dressed as nuns and the Baroness, and women dressed as Nazi's and Max Detweiler, but the raunchy element succeeds, even with family audiences, because the humor is entirely based on innuendo. For example, in the American show, there are party-poppers, and the audience is warned about the perils of premature popping. The adults get the joke on one level, and the kids relate to it on another.

In September of 2000, the official North American premiere of

Singalong Sound of Music took place in New York City, and the organizers invited me to come along. Dan Truhitte (Rolf) also came to town for the premiere and during an interview together, I got an unexpected treat. We sang "Sixteen Going on Seventeen" together for the first time since 1964, and joked about how we should change the words, because neither of us can claim to be even close to sixteen or seventeen anymore.

Ironically, *The Today Show* was again the program that launched the event nationwide. The day of the premiere just happened to coincide with an on-the-air wedding that had been in the planning stages for months. *The Today Show* audience had actually selected the bride and groom out of four couples (who were already engaged), and had also chosen everything for the wedding, from the dresses and tuxes, to the food that would be eaten at the brunch, to the location of the honeymoon.

The result of bringing *Singalong* promoters together with a traditional Jewish wedding was hysterical. Tom Lightburn, *Singalong's* producer, arrived dressed as a nun with a "Sound of Music" banner draped around his neck. "There I was," he told me, "Attending my first Jewish wedding, standing in the middle of Manhattan outside Rockefeller Center, trying to adjust my whimper." It was perfect.

He wasn't the only one who was 'into it' that day. I'll always remember when I saw the men who worked for Twentieth Century Fox who were in town for not only the premiere of *Singalong*, but also the release of the DVD and CD of *The Sound of Music*. Unbeknownst to me, the studio had made them lederhosen costumes out of drapes. I turned around at the theater to find these four grown men, wearing costumes identical to the ones that Nicky and Duane had worn during the filming of "Do-Re-Mi", and I just about fell over, laughing.

The audience's costumes were amazing. As always, there were nuns and Nazi's and Gretl's and Friedrich's. Three people were dressed as "winters that melt into spring", starting with snow atop their heads, and ending with spring flowers on their shoes. The creativity involved was inspiring. The person who won the costume contest was "sixteen-going-on-seventeen" and "seventeen-going-on-eighteen." On one side of his body, he was dressed as Liesl, and on the other side was dressed as Rolf.

Dear Charmy,

When you go to 'Singalong', do you dress up? If you wore a costume, who would you be?

I've never gone in costume, but if I did, there's only one character I would play: Liesl. There's no other character or 'thing' in the film I'd rather be. In fact, if I could just borrow my gazebo dress, I'd be all set.

I loved that dress. Designed by award-winning costume designer Dorothy Jeakins, I heard not too long ago that it was purchased in an auction and is now in a museum in Texas. While I don't think *I'm* quite ready to be put in a museum yet, I'd sure love to have that dress to wear to *Singalong*. I think each person needs to find the costume which suits them best.

My mum took me to see the film when I was nine and I drove the rest of my family crazy singing "The Lonely Goatherd" over and over again.

I went last week to see Singalonga. *2,000 people were dressed as characters from the film, including 20 women dressed as the Alps. One even had a Barbie-sized Sister Maria nun on her Alpine shoulder.*

I'm going again with 19 other friends who are equally eager to dress up and sing along with you and the rest of the cast. It's a secret what I'm going as, but I'll tell you. The goat, of course!

Until *Singalong Sound of Music*, I had only seen the complete film nine times. Even when my co-author and editor on <u>Forever Liesl</u> tried to cajole me into watching it with them while the book was in production, I declined. But in just three months this past year, I saw *The Sound of Music* three times while attending *Singalong* performances in Austin, New York, and London, and I'll be the first in line to see it yet again. I've heard from many fans who will do likewise.

I have seen Singalong Sound of Music at the Ziegfeld in Manhattan two times already, and I'm going again tomorrow. It is so inspiring... my first time to see the film on the big screen after being a lifelong fan. To be able to see it in a huge theater with a giant screen and audience participation was indescribable...

It started in 1998 and was only supposed to play for one night, in an old movie theater in London. Now, over two years later, *Singalonga Sound of Music* continues its run, selling out to crowds night after night, not only in London, but in theaters around the world.

As a young girl, I remember riding my bicycle almost half a mile to the local theater to see The Sound of Music *again and again. I have four children of my own now, and my nine year old daughter shares my love of music and song. Two weeks ago, we went to New York City to participate in* Singalong. *It was a fun, amazing, joyful afternoon that will never be forgotten.*

I had not seen the film on a large screen for many years. I wish you could have seen the audience, from babes in arms to older couples, following every word. You and the film are still an inspiration to more people than you will ever know.

Some people say it's sacrilegious. But what I've experienced has been the opposite of that. The passion and love the audience members bring to the theater is infectious. I hope that, like *The Sound of Music* itself, *Singalonga* is around for a very long time.

Inspiration

As I walk across the pedestrian bridge that spans the Salzach River, I am struck by a memory. Fans who travel to Salzburg recognize the bridge as the one that the children run across with Fraulein Maria, pointing excitedly up and down the river when they reach the other side. But as I walk across this bridge, I don't see "us" in my mind. I see Robert Wise, our director. As we ran across the bridge, he was thirty feet in the air, seated alongside cinematographer Ted McCord on a camera crane, and as we ran toward them, I could see Bob dropping down in front of us, directing how the camera should arc down to capture the scene.

Everywhere I turn in Salzburg, I am reminded of Robert Wise. He was responsible for making every major decision regarding *The Sound of Music*. He chose the cast, fighting hard to get not only Julie, but Chris Plummer. He chose us all, and hired the most talented people he could find in the business to work behind the camera, most importantly, Saul Chaplin, who helped him in every way imaginable. If Bob was the heart of *The Sound of Music*, Saul was its soul.

Back in Salzburg now, I am in awe of the man who stood at the helm of our movie. With adult hindsight, I have a greater appreciation of the tremendous burden that rested upon Bob's shoulders. Twentieth Century Fox's existence literally hung in the balance in 1964. The studio was either going to survive or go under based upon the success of *The Sound of Music*, and Bob bore the brunt of that weight with grace.

I think the only way he survived the pressure he was under was his ability to fall asleep whenever he had a free moment. I'd turn around on the set, and there would be Bob, dozing for a few minutes between takes, with all the noise and activity swirling around him. His ability to be completely relaxed created a wonderful environment to work in. I don't ever remember feeling tense or rushed or anxious on the set, and because of his demeanor, I was never afraid of making a mistake.

I've never met a more patient man in my life. Quiet and unassuming, never mercurial or maniacal like one might envision a director of his level of success would be, he waited calmly until he got every scene shot exactly the way he wanted it. He never screamed or yelled. He just said softly, "Let's do it again", and we did, until it was perfect. I believe his gift of knowing when something was 'cooked to perfection' is the reason the film is so flawless and has stood up so well over time.

During the nine months we worked together, Bob became more than a director and a mentor: he became a surrogate father. He was so different from my own father. My dad was a musician, and music was (and still is) his life, to the exclusion of almost everything else. By example, Bob Wise taught me that a man could be loyal and consistent and sympathetic. More than once, he helped guide and support me, not only when we were making *The Sound of Music*, but in all the years that have followed. He helped shape my adult life. I've learned he has helped shape many lives.

When I was eight years old, I wrote a letter to Robert Wise asking for his advice on getting into the movies. I can't believe I did this now (as if he had nothing else to do but answer letters from kids). I still have the letter he wrote me in reply. As a child, I just accepted it. But now, as an adult, I realize how absolutely kind it was for him to have written me and I cherish the letter. The movie is truly inspiring to me - like Robert Wise. What a wonderfully thoughtful man...

I couldn't agree more. Through the years, as I've watched Bob age along with me, he has been an inspiration, always. A true gentleman within the film world, never flirtatious, always professional, his personal values are reflected in his film-making efforts. I don't believe he knows how special he is, or how deeply his films affect people. So many have written to tell me that *The Sound of Music* not only entertained them: it inspired.

The Sound of Music *has been my favorite movie for 35 years. I was in the first grade when it premiered in 1965, and I still recall with delight being taken to the old Nixon Theater in downtown Pittsburgh to see it - reserved seats, huge screen and all! I really took to heart the message Maria learned at the Abbey that the most important thing for me to do in life was to find the will of God and do it wholeheartedly.*

I graduated from college and entered the seminary to study for the Roman Catholic priesthood. One month after I began my studies, I had the opportunity to meet the real Maria von Trapp when she came to speak at a local parish church. What a thrill that was!

When I was ordained, the priest who spoke at my first Mass based his homily upon The Sound of Music. *I was so happy to be able to acknowledge the great part this wonderful story played in my own religious vocation...*

The Sound of Music has helped people discover their true calling, their life work. One woman told me how profoundly the film influenced her. From the first time she watched it as a child, she was in love with musicals, ultimately deciding to pursue the study of musical theater. When she was required to write an essay for her college application, she wrote about *The Sound of Music* and the joy it has brought to her life. She was accepted by the Boston Conservatory.

She is not the only person whose future was influenced by the movie.

The Sound of Music *played an integral part in my hope as a child in Michigan and was ultimately an inspiration for my long career in show business, working with young television actors. My gift of teaching, influencing, and instilling hope in young people is very dear to me...*

Of course, Bob wasn't the only one responsible for inspiring all these people. Other exceptional individuals played key roles in making *The Sound of Music* a source of inspiration, most particularly Richard Rodgers and Oscar Hammerstein II. Millions have been transformed by the wonderful songs they wrote.

> *I was three when* The Sound of Music *was released. The film and its music shaped my brother's and my development to an untold degree. I recall listening to the soundtrack album unceasingly while growing up and those performances are indelibly etched in my mind's ear. Through constant repeated playing of the album, we wore out the vinyl. We are both now musicians whose love for music is rooted in our love for that special film...*

I have heard many similar stories.

> *The music alone thrilled me and made me feel better. I don't think Rodgers and Hammerstein had any idea the difference their music would make in people's lives...*

Of course, the depth of love some people have for the music has, at times, been a bit wearing on others around them.

> *When the movie came out in 1965, I was Brother Bonaventure, a Franciscan monk. Every Saturday evening, groups of Brothers would go into town to see this new movie called* The Sound of Music. *They were always asking me to go, but I would decline, in my mind assuming the movie would be boring. Well, finally one Saturday I consented. As soon as the movie began, it took my breath away. I never knew such beautiful scenery existed on God's Earth. I sat spellbound, for the entire movie.*
>
> *After that I went to see the movie every time there was room in the car. And I got the soundtrack. I made one of my superiors, Brother Edward, sick of hearing the music because I played it so often. One afternoon, during recreation, I was in my room quietly playing the soundtrack, when he barged in, took the record, put it in its jacket, and flung it out the window. It landed eight feet below on the kitchen roof. Needless to say I had to get a ladder to retrieve it...*

I have this wonderful image in my mind of Brother Bonaventure, teetering on the ladder, rescuing his soundtrack. Perhaps Brother Edward couldn't understand why he was so enthralled by this music, but many people around the world would.

This film has been with me my whole life. It is embedded in my heart and soul. I first saw it in Malta, as a little girl of five or six, and then again, when I was twelve, at school (a convent school - what an atmosphere!)

The songs I have heard over and over and over and I have sung them to practically every little child I have ever known, making sure that the music and songs are never forgotten, keeping up the tradition of passing them on to the next generation, filling this world with the sound of music...

Rodgers and Hammerstein changed the world with their music, but I doubt they ever realized the full extent of their legacy. Oscar Hammerstein II died four years before the film was even made. I wish he could have lived to see it, to see how the canvas of the film further enhanced his lyrics, and to witness how the world responded to *The Sound of Music* when it was first released. As more than one fan has pointed out, 1965 was a time when the world needed a wonderful story.

Thanks for all the joy you and the other cast members brought to the United States, as well as the rest of the world. After the tragedy of President Kennedy, we needed an uplifting, and you did it...

Seeing the film for the first time was a powerful experience.

I was thirteen in 1965 when I saw the film at Radio City Music Hall with my class. That scene of "Do-Re-Mi" on the mountain was a spiritual experience: an explosion of energy, Divine Love, within my heart. I had to grip the chair arms to stop myself from plunging into the screen and joining you...

Many were too young to be able to articulate why the film touched their hearts. All they knew was they loved it. Their understanding of why would come much later.

I was only 3 when the movie came out, but I was entranced by it from the first time I saw it. At 3 you don't understand why this is, it's something that's just there.
It's what the movie stands for that touches me now - having confidence in yourself, having a good family relationship, the power of music, and having the courage to stand up for what you believe in, even if it goes against what others 'believe' is right. The Sound of Music - it's almost a little reminder from God as to what our priorities in life need to be...

While some people are most affected by the music, others have found a deep resonance simply with the scenery of the film. Those magnificent Austrian vistas have even influenced where some people choose to live.

I grew up in Northern New Jersey, not far from NYC. Throughout my childhood, I remember longing to live in the countryside and the mountains. If I saw such scenery in a magazine, it stopped me cold. So you can imagine how I felt when I saw the movie. So many things that were already a part of my personality came out through the screen; I felt as if I had "come home". That day I made up my mind that SOMEDAY I would live in the mountains and meet wonderful people like the von Trapps. My dream came true. I moved to the Adirondacks shortly after high school and I never get tired of being in the mountains.
I feel The Sound of Music *is an attitude. I've been able to weave what I could into my real life: living in the mountains, making quality friendships. I have what I call "Sound of Music" moments, like recently when I was driving on a beautiful stretch*

of road in Vermont on a gorgeous summer day, not a cloud in the sky, alongside a bubbling brook, listening to classical music. And I thought, "Now THIS is a Sound of Music moment!"

Some people credit their sense of inspiration to Liesl.

When I was a little girl, I prided myself on being able to sing just like Liesl from The Sound of Music. *Okay, so maybe I wasn't that good. But I sure did want to be like Liesl. I wanted you to know that you were a role model for me as I grew up. I am now twenty years old and a voice major in college. May Liesl, and* The Sound of Music, *truly live on forever !*

"Liesl" had many creators, first and foremost of whom were the von Trapps themselves, particularly Rupert, the oldest child in the real family, and his sister, Agathe, the oldest daughter. Though far different from the fictional character they are linked to, Rupert and Agathe are the reason "Liesl" exists in the first place.

So is Maria von Trapp, by writing <u>The Story of the Trapp Family Singers</u>, which led German director, Wolfgang Reinhardt, to make *Die Trapp Familie*, which resulted in Howard Lindsay and Russel Crouse writing the Broadway play, *The Sound of Music*, and giving Liesl her name, and Rodgers and Hammerstein who gave her great songs to sing, and then Ernest Lehman, who enhanced her character in his screenplay, and Bob and Saul and Dee Dee and Marc who each added even more dimensions to the character that I ultimately portrayed on screen. So when people write to tell me how much they love Liesl, I always hope they know a whole team of people helped create her.

Writing my memoir gave me an opportunity to pay homage to what the character has meant to me in my life. It's been gratifying to hear how <u>Forever Liesl</u> has affected readers.

Your story touched me deeply. It is so easy sometimes to give up hope for finding love, be it from a parent or a mate. Thanks for giving all of us one more reason to believe...

Sometimes, people have stumbled across the book at just the right moment.

I'm an actress on the London stage. When I was a child, I always wanted to sing on stage, and to go on to earn a living doing what I always dreamed of was a wish come true. But hopes and dreams are funny things. The discipline involved in a long-running show makes it hard sometimes to keep the dream alive.

But today, a chest infection rendered me speechless for once in my life and this afternoon I crawled out of the house to the bookshop hoping to find inspiration to keep me from going crazy. I saw your book on The Sound of Music *and without a second thought, picked it up. I finished it a short while ago, at one in the morning.*

Reading your words made me realize the gift I was given and that it's my duty to embrace it and keep it alive. I just wanted to say thank you for inspiring me. Today you just made me want to sing for no good reason (even though I do sound like a frog at the moment) and that is so important to me...

The words this actress chose to describe her singing talent are similar to the words I would use to describe the gift of *Music* in my own life. In recent years, I have became acutely aware of what a blessing the role of Liesl has been for me and, like this actress, recognize my own responsibility to embrace this gift.

Being "Liesl" encouraged me to strive toward higher ideals in my personal and professional life. As Nicky has often said, "Living up to the image of having been in this film has made all of us try harder in every aspect of our lives." He's right. What's nice is that this effort is often acknowledged.

All of you who were involved in this magnificent movie are a testament to the remarkable people you are. Your siblings, both biological and celluloid, as well as the von Trapps themselves, are an inspiration to the rest of the world. All of you have shown that, no matter what adversity life throws at you, it is still possible to have a happy productive life. Thank you...

My immediate response to such gratitude is, it is I who am thankful to all of you. It has been my good fortune to be a part of *The Sound of Music*, and to have played a small part in its magic outreach. Yet I don't consider myself personally responsible for the deep feelings the film can evoke. Julie and Chris and Bob and Saul and Ernie deserve the majority of credit for letters like this one.

This movie has always given me a sense of belonging. It makes me feel that I will someday find my dream no matter how remote the possibility seems by reminding me that there is always hope, that if you look for your life and follow your dreams, happiness does find you, and that when you have people around who love you, nothing else matters and everything is clear.

The film's spiritual undertones can affect people every single time they watch it.

I have been a fan of The Sound of Music *since I saw it in a theater at the age of 4 (I am now 28). I watch the movie often. It is perfect accompaniment to paper grading and bad mood days. I just watched the film again the other day and found myself tearing up throughout it. I really believe that the film holds many spiritual messages, and it reminds our society that love does prevail - and we are here to help one another...*

The film has helped people in a diverse number of ways.

I work and volunteer as a physical therapist at a rehabilitation facility for the physically disabled and they are truly moved by watching this movie throughout the year. You and The Sound of Music *have brought so much joy to me and those I love...*

Sometimes, *The Sound of Music* has led to a whole new path in life. One of the most humorous letters I ever received ends with a profound new life direction.

I am now a vicar of a large, very rural parish in West Wales. Twenty years ago, when the local amateur operatic society was doing The Sound of Music, *just two weeks before the opening night, most of the back-stage staff and many of the male cast walked out after a huge row with the dictatorial producer. The woman who played Maria was a singer in my rock band, and she begged me to take over the role of the Captain, and asked my wife to help backstage.*

I nervously joined the already established cast, feeling much as you portrayed yourself when joining the film. There were the inevitable disasters, such as a very mischievous "Kurt" breaking his arm at dress rehearsal, my guitar string breaking with a very loud "twang" during the touching 'Edelweiss' scene with the children in the drawing room, and the convent 'backcloth' collapsing during the Mother Abbess's "Climb Ev'ry Mountain."

"Maria" and I could not help collapsing into totally uncontrollable giggles during the love scene. The libretto of the stage play has the Captain saying something like, "Then one night, all of a sudden, it (one's life) stands before you." To which Maria comments tenderly, "What is this great thing that comes between us?" And I was to respond, "So you have felt it too?" The double entendre implications of the dialogue rendered us both utterly and very painfully helpless and out of action with tears streaming down our faces.

Amateur societies always attract more female members than males, and so the play, with all those nuns, was a popular choice. That production of ours had I think about thirty women as nuns, including two who were very obviously pregnant beneath their habits! During one of the crossover scenes, a long line of nuns - including the pregnant ones - stretched across the stage devoutly singing "Alleluia", and the loud whisper from a gentleman in the audience was heard all over the auditorium. "My God, they're breeding in the wings!"

It was during my involvement in The Sound of Music *that I began the process of seeking ordination. The result is that I am now so fulfilled and blessed, having the pastoral care of these rural parishes as their priest.* The Sound of Music *is responsible for so many good and joyous experiences that have happened to me...*

Sometimes I receive a letter from someone whose enthusiasm for life and all the world has to offer has inspired me.

It was a damp Friday in November and I was sitting in the kitchen at home having a late breakfast. I put the radio on and heard "Sixteen Going on Seventeen" playing. My ears pricked up at once: I knew the song well; as I did with all the songs from The Sound of Music, *although I had never seen the film. The broadcaster, one of my favourites on the BBC, then said that she would later be interviewing Charmian Carr and I knew straightaway that it was Liesl.*

I was born in the year of The Sound of Music *(1965) and am the youngest of twelve children. Two of my sisters had the album, and virtually before I could talk, I was lisping to the songs, remembering the tunes almost at once.*

I wore the record out, and in 1979, when I went for the first time to Canada where I celebrated my 14th birthday, one of my presents, was a cassette of the film's soundtrack and I remembered all the words to the songs. I have been back to Canada nineteen times since, and whenever I hear "The Sound of Music", it always takes me back to that magical time, to my first visit to Canada.

I said I had never seen the film - but I've heard it loads of times. I have been blind since birth, but I, nevertheless, love the dialogue and can recognize all the voices in the film. I basically know what's happening on the screen.

When you finally came on the radio that day in November, I recognized your voice as soon as I heard it. I don't think it has changed at all. What struck me was how down-to-earth you sounded. Being blind, I have to rely on voices and I could detect how much fun you would be and how genuine you are. You spoke of your book on the program and I managed to buy a copy which my partner read aloud to me. I loved it. Later, I watched the film again with my partner. It took us five hours because I made him stop every few minutes to describe everything on the screen.

I had no idea of the visuals of the film until I heard your story. You see, it no longer mattered that I couldn't see them. You brought them alive for me. Thank you...

I once wrote that when the film inspires people, it is merely reflecting their own values, their own love. Individual reactions to the film are a simply a mirror of how people wish the world would be.

The Sound of Music *is a really binding force. Anyone who loves it magnetically attracts other fans, and I have many wonderfully good friends who I have made simply by humming along the tunes or quoting sections of the film and being overheard. I don't believe you can ever really comprehend how deeply your fans are affected by the film. I have so many things in my life which are blessings, and many of them are directly because of your portrayals of the von Trapps. I am a better, more fulfilled person because I have shared in the magic, and I can pass it on to others. Thank you for spreading the von Trapp love. Most people only get the opportunity to touch a few hearts; you have united a world.*

One can't ask more from life than that!

To Sing Once More

No one Judith, our producer, contacts knows the location. Her consultants in Salzburg say they have no idea where the mountain meadow is where we filmed the beginning of 'Do-Re-Mi'. "Just take them to one of the hills above Mondsee," she is told. "No one will no the difference. A mountain top is a mountain top."

"No," Nicky says when he hears this. "We really should go back to the actual location. It's a place called Werfen."

Judith is then able to find the driver who, in 1964, took us up into the hills to film the children's picnic with Fraulein Maria, and he knows exactly where to go.

It is the last day we are to be together. I am off to London at the end of the shoot, and the rest of our little family will soon scatter to the winds. Only Angela and Heather and Debbie are staying together for a bit longer, renting a car to explore the rest of the country. "It's going to be Thelma and Louise do Austria," Angela quips.

It isn't until we all cram into the van for the drive to Werfen that it hits me: our very special reunion is almost over. As we drive up into the hills, a myriad of emotions begin to grow inside.

Judith comments that it would be great to get some aerial shots of the surrounding countryside, like the opening shots of *The Sound of Music*. Miraculously, right after she says this, a military helicopter appears on the horizon and Judith boldly jumps out of the van and flags it down.

The crew is moving some materials, and as luck would have it, they have just completed their final run. The pilot agrees to take a cameraman aloft and says they have room for just one more person, and Judith knows, after just a week of knowing us, who should be the one to go: the adventurous one who long ago took off alone on his bicycle through the streets of Salzburg, causing everyone to panic. Duane.

I'll always remember the look on his face when she asks if he'd like to go up. Duane just beams. He has such a love of nature, of Austria, and of adventure. It is perfect for him, and spontaneously the rest of us cheer, "Yes!" He grins from ear-to-ear as he climbs aboard and the huge helicopter roars upward, the back door remaining open so the cameraman can hang out and get some footage of the hills and Alps.

Of course, as soon as the helicopter takes off, our elation for Duane turns to trepidation. Shooting aerial footage from a helicopter is not without risk. We watch as Duane disappears from sight, and it isn't until the helicopter returns to view that everyone heaves a sigh of relief.

Duane clambers down, safe and sound and ecstatic, and we continue on our way. We haven't far to go, and soon turn into an instantly recognizable meadow high above the valley and surrounded by gorgeous Alps. There is a sudden collective hush in the van. We are back.

The view at our feet is breathtaking. The green hillside dwarfed by magnificent peaks looks like an enormous outdoor cathedral. Remarkably, nothing is different. We return to find Werfen unchanged. The old barn where we went for shelter from the rain still stands. Long ago, Nicky and I had huddled in blankets inside this barn and laughed at Saul Chaplin's jokes. We walk inside now and the smell of the hay and the damp wood takes me back to the rainy afternoon when Julie and Marc and Saul had harmonized together here.

It is suddenly difficult to maintain my composure. Ghosts are with us here on this hillside. Memories of those halcyon days are bittersweet as we reflect upon the parents and friends who were with us when last we ran across this slope, yet who are no longer on this Earth. We cannot escape the passage of time or the reality that, chances are, the seven of us will not be coming back in another thirty-six years.

Debbie begins to cry, and it unleashes us all. Nicky stands looking at a tree stump nearby. "The last time I sat right here, Solly was telling me a joke. Remember how he would tell us stories about Judy Garland and all the musicals he worked on." And then Nicky's voice trails off and there are tears in his eyes. Saul is gone now. Many people are gone now.

It has been an incredible thing to make this journey together. It has given the seven of us an opportunity for an intimacy we've never been able to experience before. I feel a new, deeper, closeness with my "Sound of Music" family.

As we stand here amid this autumn beauty, I suddenly realize what is happening. Here on this hillside, we are saying goodbye to the many people who were a part of this film and are no longer with us. Here in Werfen, we will say goodbye to dreams forever lost, to our childhoods even. More than any other site we have visited, Werfen has brought us face-to-face with what *The Sound of Music,* and all the people affiliated with it, has meant to all our lives.

As children in this meadow, we sang "Do-Re-Mi". Now Judith approaches us with a different request. "Would you all be willing to sing 'So Long, Farewell'?"

With somber faces, we line up on that majestic hillside. The director begins to play a CD of the music from the soundtrack, and the seven of us begin to sing along with our own childhood voices. "There's a sad sort of clanging from the clock in the hall, and the bells in the steeple too..."

Judith films us in one take. I don't think we could have handled more than that.

Debbie can barely get the words out, she is crying so hard, and I feel myself choking up. "So long, farewell, auf Wiedersehen, goodbye..." To hear our child voices in the background only makes the moment more poignant.

So much has happened, so much time has passed. Where did it go? We were just here, after all, wearing clothes made of drapes, following Julie Andrews around this field as if she were the Pied Piper.

As each of us finishes our line in the song, we walk out of the camera frame, first Debbie, then Nicky, and then it is my turn. "I'd like to stay and taste my first champagne..."

I step away and watch as Duane sings his high note, followed by Angela and Heather, until all that is left is Kym. It is haunting for me to watch her. Here is the little girl I once carried in my arms, all grown up now, a mother, with half her life behind her. "The sun has gone to bed and so must I..."

As she steps away, it is just the mountain and the wind and our voices from long ago ending the refrain, "Goodbye...goodbye... goodbye..."

Older and Wiser

This past year, people from all over the world taught me something I didn't know: *The Sound of Music* isn't just a movie. Perhaps I should have realized this long ago, but I wasn't listening to the music. But I'm older and wiser now. I listen.

Dear Charmy,

Your movie selves will live long after all of us are gone, and will continue to inspire and uplift people everywhere. And if we ever meet beings from other planets, I am confident that your film will be one of the best things that our planet has to offer them, along with soaring violin music, sweet German chocolate, and the gorgeous mountains of Austria...

This is the truth. The film will long outlive me, outlive us all. At first, it seemed strange to think that after I'm gone, people will still be watching this movie, that I'll be forever sixteen, spinning in that gazebo. But I ultimately realized this is a great gift. When I'm no longer alive, my daughters and granddaughter, whenever they miss me, will be able to slip in a copy of the video and I'll be with them again.

All of us who were a part of the film, whether on camera or not, will have achieved a certain immortality from having been a part of it. But the legacy of *The Sound of Music* is not ours alone.

When people wrote to me back in 1965, and in the first few years that the film was out, they would express their awe at the beauty of the film, and how much it affected them. The letters I receive now are different. The film has become a part of people's lives. *The Sound of Music* has been there to cheer people up when they are down, and to keep them afloat when they face the most despairing situations. People take it with them into the delivery room for the beginning of life, and into a hospice room for the end of it. They are married to the wedding march, sing "Edelweiss" to their babies when they put them to sleep, and carry their small children to bed singing "So Long, Farewell". Boys and girls leap from couch to couch, and spin in imaginary meadows, acting out treasured fantasies. Teens dance in gazebos, dreaming of their own idealized first love, and men have gotten down on one knee to propose within a gazebo's doors. Fathers have been inspired to reach out to their children and people young and old have learned about oppression and courage.

The Sound of Music has taught people about themselves.

It is remarkable that a single movie has done this for people at every latitude and longitude on Earth. Those of us involved in the film can scarcely comprehend the ways in which 'we' have become a part of people's lives, how our faces and voices have been incorporated into people's conscious experiences. It's impossible for me to entirely absorb it all. But I feel blessed to have been a part of this film, this story. I hear the music now, and I feel a greater hand than ours was involved in this miracle.

This is what I wanted to share with my second family on our journey to Salzburg. It's what the letters to Liesl taught me: *The Sound of Music* is more than a movie. It has become a part of everyone it has ever touched.

The Sound of Music is you...

Acknowledgments

There are so many people to thank for making this second book. First and foremost, of course, is my friend, Jean Strauss, without whom Forever Liesl would not be "forever" and these letters would only be etched in my mind. I love you.

To my dear friend, Libby Agran Fitzwater, who suggested we write it, my love and thanks.

To Kim Sandmann who originally came up with the idea of the website, www.CharmianCarr.com, where many of these letters were initially sent, and to David Fuchslin who spent so much of his time making the site beautiful, my deep gratitude.

To Robert Wise, Julie Andrews, Christopher Plummer, Ernest Lehman, and Saul Chaplin's widow Betty, thank you for all your support of my book projects, and for making *The Sound of Music* such a special part of all our lives.

To Judith Holder at Granada Media, Bert Fink and Ted Chapin of the Rodgers and Hammerstein Organization, Tom Lightburn of *Singalong Sound of Music*, and Rick Rhoades of Twentieth Century Fox, who have all made the last year so much fun, my everlasting appreciation.

Several people helped provide the photographs in this book: Eileen Hammond (Nicky's mother), Debbie Larson, Angela Cartwright, Heather Menzies, Kim Sandmann, Emily Watkins, and Rebecca Herrera at Twentieth Century Fox. A picture really is worth a thousand words. And my thanks to Joel Cinnamon and Andrew Hilman who not only helped with the photographs, but who designed the most beautiful cover, ever.

I can't thank my film family enough for all their support on both of my books. Our "Sound of Music" journey will always be our bond, and so to Nicky, who has been there for me always and forever, and to Heather, Duane, Angela, Debbie and Kym, my eternal love.

And to Rachel Shiery, her mom, Sandy, her dad, Chris, and her sister Chelsea, thank you for letting me share, not only your story, but a very special afternoon.

Out of the thousands of letters I've received, Jean and I selected one hundred and sixty-four to help us tell the story of the film and its impact, worldwide. This book would not have been impossible without the enthusiasm and willingness of the following individuals: Maureen Ahlers, Kimberley Akester, Alejandro Zamudio Almada, Darryl David Amato, Alana Lafrance Anderson, Lea Anderson-Smith, Katherine and Kristel Anglo, Allan Aquino, Gregory Bandy, Lillian Beals, Eloise Beardsley, Bill Benson, Lucy Binns, Hal Boggess, Alison Bolton, Brother Bonaventure, Julie Bonno, Christopher Bradley, Liesl Bradner, Debbie Breeden, Grace Ann Brimmer, Lindsey Rose Broad, Shonali Burke, Susan Burke, John J. Carney, Patti Carpenter, Thomas Carr, Adriana Casteñeda, Kate Cerneglia, Eric Chaffey, Reverend K.M.D. Cottam, Mark S. Creech, Bernadette Crespin, Kerry Maureen Cummings, Jacqueline Thompson Cunningham, Lea Merrill Davidson, Johann D. May Deferio, Peggy Dickston, Bonnie Doucette, Chris Doyle, Greg and Suzanne Ehrbar, Tricia Endozo, Joanne Evans, Rachel Ezrine, Laurie and Geraldine Fernandez, Kristin Fitzgerald, Amie Forster, Grace Franco, Monica Friedlander, Maribeth Fullerton, Gloria Gallagher-Smith, Michele Zanca Gallagher, Laura Julia Garcia, Corrine Giacobbe, Kal Grant, Monica Grant, Marisol Villamil Greenberg, Diana Martin-Gruener, Tonia Renée Guilbault, Mark Gunter, Bob Hansen, Linda Hensley, Daniel Hernandez, Lam Pin Hien, Barb and Kelly Holmin, Brad Horner, Brenda G. Hoy, Gregory John Hunter, Keith James, Maria F. Janossy, Kari M. Jernas, Erin Jespersen, Megan Johnson, Brent Jones, Liesl Jorgensen-Almeria, Corey Karvonen-Lee, Doug Kaufman, Pinar Kobas, Elizabeth Kozak, Barrie J. Kreinik, Kristopher Kyer Antekeier, Lindsay Lackey, Anne Leedom and Maryann R. Mattos, Mark Leigh, Christine and Caleb and Katelyn Lewis, Debra Lial, Jay

Littner, Donna E. Lorusso, Lisa Marie Magedler, Jeff Marquis, Dominick Marrone, Mary Sue McAlister, Carl McDonald, Jennifer Claire McNally, Carol McNeillie, Masao Cimons Morinaga, Kathy, Travis, Emily, Jake and Robby Moss, Liesl Muckey, Angie Mueller, Walter Newkirk, Jennifer Nixon, Jeraldine M. Obien, Dawn Marie O'Brien, Carri Ogrodnik, Fiona Parker, Patricia Perry, Tony Pickens, Linda A. Pieroni-Munro, Leigh Pikarski, Allegra Pollock, Leslie D. Pursell, Catrin Richards, Cara E. Richardson, Cecily Richardson, Robin Rebecca Roberts, Robert Rocco, Rolf Rockliff, Allison Rose, Amy and Danny Rusak, Katharina Sadowski, Jeffrey Schlichter, Nancy J. S. Schott, Yelena N. Severina, Judy and Kathy Schulberg, Amy M. Shanahan, Cathy Sheagren, Hiroshi Shimizu, Benjamin Shull, Judith Ann Sicora, Robert Siegal, Kristine, Alisa and Kailey Snider, Ryan E. Speakman, Marian Faye Stanley, Father Tim P. Stein, Charmian E. Stone, Charmaine and Liesl Storm, Melissa Sturm, Niki Noriko Suzuki, S. Roy Swanson, Emily Talbott, Rob Thorne, Soren Thustrup, Marianne L. Tierney, Jeffrey M. Todd, Vince E. Trembley, Judy Tropper, Lydia Mausser Urban, Joanne-Theresa Vassallo, Mariella Vassallo, Mario, Carla and Gina Velez, Linda Vermuelen, Evelien von der Schulenburg, Lisa M. Waldrop, Rosa Lee Walsh and Max J. Jungbauer, Lou Ann Walters, Cassie White, Eduardo Wilk, Curtis Martin Wilson, Lilah and Leizl Winget, Branch Woodman, Bill Wright, Liesl Yamaguchi, and Dona J. Yeskoo.

And last but not least, there is my family, who has stuck by me through the years, and who have made the ride worthwhile. To Jennifer and Emily, Erik and Grant, Emma, Jay, Sharon, Darleen and Jameson, I love you.

And to all of you who have inspired me through the years with your letters, making me laugh and making me cry, know how much you have also made 'the ride' a true pleasure. You make the world a better place. Please come back and visit me at www.CharmianCarr.com...

List of Illustrations

Cover

Werfen, 1964.
Charmian Carr's personal collection.

Frontpiece

Chicago, 1947.
Photo by Rita Oehman Farnon.

One word for Each Note

With co-author, Jean Strauss.
Jean Strauss personal collection.

Homeward Bound

With Nicholas, Heather, Duane,
Angela, Debbie and Kym in Chicago,
en route to Austria.
Photo from Debbie Turner Larson.

Something Good

Salzburg, 1964. Bottom (l-r) Duane,
Debbie, Kym, Angela. Top (l-r)
Heather, Nicholas, Charmian.
Photo by Eileen Hammond

On the Road with Liesl

Fox "Music" European tour, 1966.
Charmian Carr private collection.

The Liesl Club

With Kelly McLean in Palm Desert.
Photo by Kim Sandmann.

Bachelor Dandies

With Nicholas Hammond, c. 1990.
Photo by Jay Brent.

Gazebo Dancers

With Dan Truhitte in rehearsal, 1964.
Courtesy of the Twentieth Century
Fox Film Corporation.

Thunderstorms

With Rachel Shiery, November, 2000.
Photo by Jean Strauss.

Family	Charmian with her daughters, Emily Watkins (l) and Jennifer Svensson (r), and her Labradors, Wilson, Amber and Molly. Photo by Jay Brent.
The Human Spirit	With the Trapp family in Stowe, Vermont. From left to right: Maria, Debbie, Werner, Charmian, Johannes, Agathe, Rosmarie, and Duane. Photo by Emily Watkins.
The Children	With the cast of *The Sound of Music*, Sonoma California, 2000. Courtesy of Broadway Bound's Suzanne Duran. Photo by Jean Strauss.
Friends Around the World	In Salzburg: Kym, Debbie, Angela, Duane, Heather, Nicholas, Charmian. Photo by Angela Cartwright.
Singalonga	At New York premiere with (l-r) Rick Rhoades, Keith Kaminski, and Jon Schafer. Photo anon.
Inspiration	With Robert Wise. Photo by Jay Brent.
To Sing Once More	At Werfen: Debbie, Nicholas, Charmy, Duane, Angela, Heather and Kym. Photo by Heather Menzies.
Older and Wiser	Charmy w/her granddaughter Emma. Photo by Jay Brent.
Acknowledgments	In Salzburg: Charmy, Angela, Duane, Debbie, Heather, Kym, Nicholas. Photo by Angela Cartwright.
Endpiece	Salzburg, 1964. Private collection, Charmian Carr.

The Authors

Charmian Carr was born in Chicago in December of 1942 and made her film debut in *The Sound of Music* in 1965. Her other credits include Stephen Sondheim's *Evening Primrose* with Anthony Perkins and *A & E's Rodgers and Hammerstein: The Sound of Movies*, as well as over two hundred television commercials.

A mother, grandmother, interior designer, and co-author of *Forever Liesl: A Memoir of "The Sound of Music"*, she makes her home in Encino, California with her two yellow Labradors, Wilson and Amber.

Jean Strauss, a graduate of UC Berkeley and USC, has two sons and lives in southern California where her husband is a college president. In addition to co-authoring *Forever Liesl* with Charmian Carr, she has also written *Beneath a Tall Tree*, *Birthright: The Guide to Search and Reunion*, and *The Great Adoptee Searchbook*.

Quick Order Form

Fax orders: 909-625-1040. Copy and send this form.

Email orders: www.arete-usa.com

Postal orders: Arete Publishing Company of America
                    P.O. Box 127, Claremont, CA 91711 USA

Letters to Liesl Price: $15.00 US $22.50 CAN

The book is personally autographed by Charmian Carr when purchased through Arete-USA. For a personal inscription, add $5 handling, and please write below how you would like the inscription to read. Allow an extra four weeks for delivery.

_____

_____

Name:_____

Address:_____

_____

City: _____ State_____ Zip_____-_____

Telephone:_____

Email:_____

Sales tax: Add 8% tax for products shipped within California.

Shipping:
USA: $5 for the first book and $2 for each additional copy. All books shipped US Priority Mail.
International: $12 for the first book and $4 for each additional copy.

Payment: Check   Credit card
     Visa   MasterCard   AMEX   Discover

Card number:_____

Name on card:_____Exp. Date:___/___